THE NEW
TESTAMENT

PAULINE REVELATION
COMPANION

HOLY
BIBLE

LARGE PRINT

KING JAMES VERSION
TRANSLATION

Compiled by Robert E. Daley

First Edition — February 2014

Published by: The Larry Czerwonka Company, LLC
thelarryczerwonkacompany.com

Printed in the United States of America

ISBN: 0615968775
ISBN-13: 978-0615968773

The Larry Czerwonka Company, LLC
Hilo, Hawai'i

Great and manifold were the blessings, most dread Sovereign, which Almighty God, the Father of all mercies, bestowed upon us the people of *England*, when first he sent Your Majesty's Royal Person to rule and reign over us. For whereas it was the expectation of many, who wished not well unto our *Sion*, that, upon the setting of that bright *Occidental Star*, Queen *Elizabeth*, of most happy memory, some thick and palpable in doubt which way they were to walk, and that it should hardly be known who was to direct the unsettled State; the appearance of Your Majesty, as of the *Sun* in his strength, instantly dispelled those supposed and surmised mists, and gave unto all that were well affected exceeding cause of comfort; especially when we beheld the Government established in Your Highness, and Your hopeful Seed, by an undoubted Title; and this also accompanied with peace and tranquility at home and abroad.

But among all our joys, there was no one that more filled our hearts than the blessed continuance of the preaching of God's sacred Word among us, which is that inestimable treasure, which excelleth all the riches of the earth; because the fruit thereof extendeth itself, not only to the time spent in this transitory world, but directeth and disposeth men unto that eternal happiness which is above in heaven.

Then not to suffer this to fall to the ground, but rather to take it up, and to continue it in that state wherein the famous Predecessor of Your Highness did leave it; nay, to go forward with the confidence and resolution of a man, in maintaining the truth of Christ, and propagating it far and near, is that which hath Then not to suffer this to fall to the ground, but rather to take it up, and to continue it in that state wherein the famous Predecessor of Your Highness did leave it; nay, to go forward with the confidence and resolution of a man, in maintaining the truth of Christ, and so bound and firmly knit the hearts of all Your Majesty's loyal and religious people unto You, that Your very name is precious among them: their eye doth behold You with comfort, and they bless You in their hearts, as that sanctified Person, who, under God, is the immediate author of their true happiness. And this their contentment doth not diminish or decay, but every day increaseth and taketh strength, when they observe that the zeal of Your Majesty toward the house of God doth not slack or go backward, but is more and more kindled, manifesting itself abroad in the farthest parts of *Christendom*, by writing in defence of the truth (which hath given such a blow unto that Man of Sin as will not be healed) and every day at home, by religious and learned discourse, by frequenting the house of God, by hearing the Word preached, by cherishing the teachers thereof, by caring for the Church, as a most tender and loving nursing Father.

There are infinite arguments of this right Christian and religious affection in Your Majesty, but none of more forcible to declare it to others than the vehement and perpetuated desire of accomplishing and publishing this work, which now, with all humility, we present unto Your Majesty. For when Your Highness had once, out of deep judgment, apprehended how convenient it was, that, out of the Original sacred Tongues, together with comparing of the labours, both in our own and other foreign languages, of many worthy men who went before us, there should be one more exact translation of the Holy Scriptures into the *English* tongue; Your Majesty did never desist to urge and to excite those to whom it was commended, that the Word might be hastened and that the business might be expedited in so decent a manner as a matter of such importance might justly require.

And now at last, by the mercy of God, and the continuance of our labours, it being brought unto such a conclusion, as that we have great hopes that the Church of *England* shall reap good fruit thereby, we hold it our duty to offer it to Your Majesty, not only as to our King and Sovereign, but as to the principal mover and author of the Work; humbly craving of your most Sacred Majesty, that, since things of this quality have ever been subject to the censures of ill-meaning and discontented persons, it may receive approbation and patronage from so learned and judicious a Prince as Your Highness is; whose allowance and acceptance of our labours shall more honour and encourage us, than all the calumniations and hard interpretations of other men shall dismay us. So that if, on the one side, we shall be traduced by Popish persons at home or abroad, who therefore will malign us, because we are poor instruments to make Gods' holy truth to be yet more and more known unto the people, who they desire still to keep in ignorance and darkness: or if, on the other side, we shall be maligned by self-conceited brethren, who run their own ways, and give liking unto nothing but what is framed by themselves, and hammered on their anvil, we may rest secure, supported within by the truth and innocency of a good conscience, having walked the ways of simplicity and integrity, as before the Lord, and sustained without by the powerful protection of Your Majesty's grace and favour, which will ever give countenance to honest and Christian endeavours against bitter censures and uncharitable imputations.

The Lord of heaven and earth bless Your Majesty with many and happy days: that, as his heavenly hand hath enriched Your Highness with many singular and extraordinary graces, so You may be the wonder of the world in this latter age for happiness and true felicity, to the honor of that great God, and the good of his Church, through Jesus Christ our Lord and only Saviour.

INTRODUCTION

This is an independent work, utilizing the King James Translation of the Bible, and the interweaving of enhancement from the compiler of this work, along with punctuation adjustment, to bring clarity concerning doctrine and expressed intended thought in line with the whole of the Pauline Revelation.

All Scripture in **BOLD PRINT** is the KING JAMES VERSION TRANSLATION of the Bible.

All Normal *ITALISIZED* PRINT is Enhancement from the compiler of this work.

Whenever a Scriptural statement from the Old Testament is made the reference is given.

The books compiled in this work are those authored by the Apostle Paul's traveling companion Luke, James and Jude the half- brothers of Jesus, John the Beloved, and the Apostle Peter.

Any alteration to punctuation,
capitalization, or original translator added
words, is in line with the
intended revelation thought.

It is the prayer of the compiler
of this work that the enhancement of
interweaving Biblical revelation truth into
each book will bring clarity for the reader
concerning who one is in Christ.

STATEMENT OF THE
PAULINE REVELATION REALITY

Within the plan that was established by
Almighty God, the Creator of this universe,
from *before the beginning* of time—the Second
Covenant, **New Creation Project** of today,
affords any Human Being, from any kindred
and tongue, living in any nation on the planet,
the opportunity to become a: ***"Born-Again,
Immortal, Recreated, Supernatural,
Resurrected, Incorruptible, Empowered-by
the-Holy-Spirit, Redeemed, More-Than-a-
Conqueror, Seated-at-the-Right-Hand,
Blood-Related, Conformed to God-in-the-
Flesh, Administrative, Household Member
of the Family of the Most High God."***

NOTABLE QUOTATIONS:

"The Bible is no mere book, but a Living Creature, with a power that conquers all that oppose it."   *Napoleon*

"That book accounts for the supremacy of England."
Queen Victoria

"It is impossible to rightly govern the world without God and the Bible."   *George Washington*

"I believe the Bible is the best gift God has ever given to man. All the good from the Saviour of the world is communicated to us through this book."   *Abraham Lincoln*

"If there is anything in my thoughts or style to commend, the credit is due to my parents for instilling me an early love of the Scriptures. If we abide by the principles taught in the Bible, our country will go on prospering and to prosper; but if we and our posterity neglect its instructions and authority, no man can tell how sudden a catastrophe may overwhelm us and bury all our glory in profound obscurity."   *Daniel Webster*

"The Bible is worth all other books which have ever been printed."   *Patrick Henry*

"The Bible is the sheet-anchor of our liberties."   *U.S. Grant*

"In all my perplexities and distresses, the Bible has never failed to give me light and strength."   *Robert E. Lee*

"The New Testament is the very best book that ever was or ever will be know in the world."   *Charles Dickens*

"I have known ninety-five of the world's great men in my time, and of these eighty-seven were followers of the Bible. The

Bible is stamped with a Specialty of Origin, and an immeasurable distance separate it from all competitors."

W.E. Gladstone

"There are more sure marks of authenticity in the Bible than in any profane history."

Sir Isaac Newton

"So great is my veneration for the Bible that the earlier my children begin to read it the more confident will be my hope that they will prove useful citizens of their country and respectable members of society. I have for many years made it a practice to read through the Bible once every year."

John Quincy Adams

"That book, sir, is the rock on which our republic rests."

Andrew Jackson

"The Bible is the truest utterance that ever came by alphabetic letters from the soul of man, through which, as through a window divinely opened, all men can look into the stillness of eternity, and discern in glimpses their far-distant, long-forgotten home."

Thomas Carlyle

"It is impossible to enslave mentally or socially a Bible-reading people. The principles of the Bible are the ground-work of human freedom."

Horace Greeley

"The existence of the Bible, as a book for the people, is the greatest benefit which the human race has ever experienced. Every attempt to belittle it is a crime against humanity."

Immanuel Kant

"The whole hope of human progress is suspended on the ever growing influence of the Bible."

W.H. Seward

Contents

Contents

THE BOOK OF
ACTS

CHAPTER 1

1. The former treatise, *which is the Gospel of Luke,* have I made, O Theophilus, of all *of the things* that Jesus began both to do and *to* teach.

2. Until the *very* day in *the* which he was taken up *from us into heaven,* after that he, through the *anointing of the* Holy Ghost, had given *final instructions and* commandments unto the apostles whom he had chosen *and who walked with him while he ministered on this earth.*

3. To whom also he showed himself *to be* alive *once again* after his passion, by many infallible proofs. Being seen of them *several times during the next* forty days, and speaking *to them* of the things pertaining to the kingdom of God.

4. And, being assembled together with **them** *on the Mount of Olivet,* commanded them that they should not depart from Jerusalem, but "Wait for the promise of the Father, which", saith he, "ye have heard of me.

5. For John *the Baptist* truly baptized *you* with water, but ye shall be baptized *by me* with the Holy Ghost not many days hence."

6. *So* when they therefore were come together, they asked of him, saying Lord, wilt thou at this time restore again the kingdom to *our Nation of* **Israel?**

7. And he said unto them, "It is not for you to know *right now* the times or the seasons, which the Father *in heaven* hath put *with*in his own power.

8. But ye shall receive *supernatural* power *yourselves*, after that the Holy Ghost is come upon you *like a cloak*. And ye shall be *living* witnesses unto me *and to what I have done* both in Jerusalem, and in all Judea, and in Samaria, and unto the uttermost part of the earth."

9. And when he had spoken these things *unto them*, while they *yet* beheld *him*, he was taken up *into heaven*, and a cloud received him out of their sight.

10. And while they looked steadfastly toward heaven as he went up, behold, two *holy angels which looked like* men stood by them in white apparel.

11. Which also said *unto them*, Ye men of Galilee, why stand ye *here* gazing up into heaven? This same *New Creation* **Jesus,** which is *just been* **taken up from you into heaven, shall so come** *back again* **in like manner as ye have seen him go into heaven.**

12.   **Then returned they unto Jerusalem from the mount called Olivet, which is from Jerusalem a** *two thousand cubit* **sabbath day's journey.**

13.   **And when they were come in, they went** *directly* **up into an upper room, where** *they all then* **abode.** *It was* **both Peter, and James, and John, and Andrew, Philip, and Thomas, Bartholomew, and Matthew, James** *the son* **of Alpheus, and Simon Zelotes, and Judas** *the brother* **of James.**

14.   **These all continued with one accord in prayer and supplication, with the women** *which followed and ministered unto Jesus,* **and** *with* **Mary the mother of Jesus, and with his** *own family* **brethren.**

15.   **And in those days Peter stood up in the midst of the** *assembled* **disciples, and said, (the number of** *the* **names** *of all those gathered* **together were about a hundred and twenty),**

16.   **Men** *and* **brethren, this Scripture** *in Psalms 41* **must needs have been fulfilled, which the Holy Ghost** *himself* **by the mouth**

of *the psalmist* David spake before concerning Judas *Iscariot,* which was *the* guide to them that took Jesus *from the Garden of Gethsemane.*

17.   For he was numbered with us *while we walked with Jesus,* and had *fully* obtained *a* part of this ministry.

18.   Now this *same* man purchased a field *of land, after he had tried to return the blood money to the Pharisees in the temple,* with the *very* reward of *his* iniquity. And *after being swallowed up with overmuch sorrow, and hanging himself, and remaining suspended on the tree over a period of time, finally* falling headlong, he burst asunder *with*in the midst *of himself,* and all *of* his bowels gushed out.

19.   And it was *commonly* known unto all *of* the dwellers at Jerusalem. Insomuch as that *particular* field is called, in their proper tongue, Aceldama, that is to say, The field of blood.

20.   For it is *also* written in the book of Psalms, *within Psalm 109,* "Let his habitation be desolate, and let no man dwell therein. And, His bishopric let another take." *(Psalms 109:6-13)*

21.   Wherefore of these men which have companied with us all *of* the time that the Lord Jesus went in and out among us,

22. Beginning from the baptism of *repentance of* John, unto that same day that he was taken up *into heaven* from us, must *there* one be ordained to be a witness *also* with us of his resurrection *from the dead.*

23. And they appointed two *individuals,* Joseph called Barsabas, who was *also* surnamed Justus, and Matthias.

24. And they *then* prayed, and said, Thou, O Lord, which knowest the hearts of all men, show *unto us* whether of these two *men that* thou hast chosen.

25. That he may take *a* part of this ministry and apostleship, from which Judas *Iscariot* by *deception and* transgression fell, that he might *fulfill the Scripture and* go to his own place *within the Abode of Damnation.*

26. And they gave forth their lots, and the lot fell upon Matthias. And he was numbered with the *other* eleven apostles.

CHAPTER 2

1. And when the day of *the Feast of* Pentecost was fully come, they were all with one accord in one place.

2. And suddenly there came a *loud* sound

from heaven as of a rushing mighty wind, and it filled all the house where they were sitting.

3. And there *visibly* appeared unto them *as it were* cloven tongues like as of fire, and it sat upon each *one* of them.

4. And they were all filled with the *anointing power of the* Holy Ghost, and *each one of them* began to speak with other tongues, as the *Holy* Spirit *of God* gave them utterance.

5. And there were dwelling at *that time in* Jerusalem, Jews *who were* devout men *of God, coming* out of every nation under heaven *to honour the Law of Moses and attend unto the Feast of Pentecost.*

6. Now when this *Holy Spirit baptism event* was noised abroad, the *whole* multitude came together *from the temple area*, and were confounded, because that every man *from various nations* heard them speak *the praises of God* in his own *native* language.

7. And they were all amazed *at this phenomena* and marveled, saying one to another, Behold, are not all of these *individuals* which speak Galileans?

8. And how *then* hear we *them*, every man *from every nation* in his own *native* tongue, wherein we were *originally* born?

9.   *We are* **Parthians, and Medes, and Elamites,** and the dwellers in **Mesopotamia.** And *we are* in **Judea** and **Cappadocia,** *and* in **Pontus** and **Asia,**

10.   **Phrygia, and Pamphylia.** *Also* in **Egypt, and in the parts of Libya about Cyrene, and strangers of Rome.** *Both* **Jews and proselytes,**

11.   **Cretes and Arabians; we do hear them speak in our** *own native* **tongues the wonderful works of God.**

12.   **And they were all amazed, and were in doubt** *as to what was happening,* **saying one to another, What meaneth this?**

13.   **Others mocking** *the move and power of God* **said, These men are full of new wine.**

14.   **But** *Simon* **Peter, standing up with the** *other* **eleven, lifted up his voice, and said unto them, Ye men of Judea, and** *all* **ye that dwell at Jerusalem, be this known unto you, and hearken** *un***to my words.**

15.   **For these individuals are not drunken** *with wine,* **as ye** *might* **suppose, seeing it is** *but morning and only* **the third hour of the day.**

16. **But this is** *the fulfillment of* **that which was spoken** *of* **by the prophet Joel.**

17.   **"And it shall come to pass in the last days," saith God, "I will pour out of my** *own*

Holy **Spirit upon all flesh** *that is on the earth.* **And your sons and your daughters shall prophesy** *by my Spirit,* **and your young men shall see visions, and your old men shall dream dreams.**

18.   **And on my servants and on my handmaidens I will pour out in those days of my Spirit, and they shall prophesy.**

19.   **And I will show wonders in** *the* **heaven above, and signs in the earth beneath; blood, and fire, and vapour of smoke.**

20.   *And* **the sun shall be turned into darkness, and the moon into** *looking like* **blood, before that great and notable day of the Lord** *is* **come.**

21.   **And it shall come to pass,** ***that*** *in that day* **whosoever shall call** *up***on the name of the Lord shall be saved."** *(Joel 2:28-32)*

22.   **Ye men of Israel, hear these words** *that I speak unto you.* **Jesus of Nazareth,** *is* **a man** *from Galilee that was* **approved of God among you by** *the* **miracles and wonders and signs, which God did by him in the midst of you** *all,* **as ye yourselves also know.**

23.   **Him, being delivered** *unto his enemies* **by the determinate counsel and foreknowledge of** *the living* **God, ye have taken, and by** *your* **wicked hands have crucified and slain.**

24.   Whom God hath *since* raised up *from the dead,* having loosed *him from* the *torment and* pains of *spiritual and physical* death. Because it was not possible that he should be holden of it *once the claims of eternal justice were satisfied.*

25.   For *the psalmist* David speaketh concerning him: "I foresaw the Lord always before my face, for he is on my right hand, that I should not be moved.

26.   Therefore did my heart rejoice, and my tongue was *exceeding* glad. Moreover also my flesh shall rest in hope,

27.   Because thou wilt not leave my soul in hell, neither wilt thou suffer thine Holy One to see corruption.

28.   Thou hast made known to me the ways of *abundant* life. Thou shalt make me full of joy with thy countenance." *(Psalms 16:8-11)*

29.   Men *and* brethren, let me freely speak unto you of the patriarch David, that he is both dead and buried, and his sepulchre is with us unto this *very* day.

30.   Therefore being a *true* prophet *of God,* and knowing that God had sworn with an oath to him, that of the fruit of his loins, according to the flesh, he would raise up *the* Christ to sit on his throne.

31. He, *prophetically* seeing this *event* before*hand*, spake of the resurrection of Christ *Jesus*, that his soul was not *to be* left in *the torment compartment of* hell, *known of as Sheol*, neither his *physical* flesh did see corruption *within the sepulchre.*

32. This *same* Jesus hath God raised up *from the dead*, whereof we all are witnesses *unto this truth.*

33. Therefore being *now* by the right hand of God *and* exalted, and having received of the Father the promise of the Holy Ghost, he hath shed forth this *phenomena*, which ye now see and hear.

34. For *when* David *speaketh forth these things he* is not *yet* ascended into the heavens. But *none the less* he saith himself: "The LORD said unto my Lord, Sit thou on my right hand,

35. Until I make thy foes *to be* thy footstool." *(Psalms 110:1)*

36. Therefore let all the house of Israel know assuredly, that God *the Father in heaven* hath made that same Jesus, whom ye have crucified *and murdered*, both *the* Lord and *the* Christ *of God.*

37. Now when they heard *this*, they were pricked *down deep* in their heart, and said

unto *Simon* **Peter** and to the rest of the apostles, **Men** *and* **brethren, what shall we** *thus* **do?**

38.   Then Peter said unto them, Repent, and be *water* baptized every one of you, in the name of Jesus Christ, for the remission of sins. And *when ye do* ye shall receive the gift *from God the Father of the indwelling* of the Holy Ghost.

39.   For the promise *of eternal life* is *made* unto you, and to your children, and to all *individuals* that are afar off, *even* as many *people* as the Lord our God shall call.

40.   And with many other words did he testify and exhort, saying, *For the love of the Lord* save yourselves from this untoward generation.

41.   Then they that gladly received his word were *indeed water* baptized *with John's baptism of repentance.* And the same *Feast* day *of Pentecost* there were added *unto them that believe* about three thousand souls.

42.   And they *all* continued steadfastly in the apostles doctrine, and *in* fellowship, and in breaking of bread *together*, and in prayers.

43.   And *the* fear *of God* came upon every soul. And many wonders and *supernatural* signs were done by the apostles.

44. And all *the Jews* that believed were *gathered* together, and had all things *in* common.

45. And *they* sold their possessions and goods, and parted them to all men, as every man had *a* need.

46. And they *all*, continuing *on a* daily *basis* with one accord *were* in the temple. And, breaking bread *with one another* from house to house, did eat their meat with gladness and singleness of heart.

47. Praising God *continually*, and having favour with all *of* the people. And the Lord added to the church daily such as should be saved.

CHAPTER 3

1. Now *on a given day* Peter and John went up together into the temple at the *time of the* hour of prayer, *being* the ninth *hour.*

2. And a certain man *who was* lame from his mother's womb was carried, whom they laid daily at the gate of the temple which is called *the* Beautiful *Gate*, to ask alms of *all* them that entered into the temple *through that gate.*

3. Who, *upon* seeing Peter and John about to go into the temple, asked *of them* an alms.

4. And Peter, fastening his eyes upon him *along* with John, said *under the direction of the Holy Spirit*, Look on us.

5. And he gave heed unto them, expecting to receive something *of value* of them.

6. Then Peter said, Silver and gold *coin* have I none *of*, but such as I have give I *unto* thee. In the name of *the New Creation* Jesus Christ of Nazareth rise up *upon your feet* and walk.

7. And he took him by the right hand, and lifted *him* up. And immediately *both of* his feet, and *his* ankle bones *as well*, received strength.

8. And he leaping up stood *on his feet*, and walked, and entered *along* with them *as they went* into the temple. *And he was* walking, and leaping, and praising God *for his mercy*.

9. And all *of* the people *that were there* saw him walking and praising God.

10. And they knew that it was he which *had* sat *and begged* for alms at the Beautiful gate of the temple. And they were *all* filled

with wonder and amazement at the *miracle* which had *just* happened unto him.

11.   And as the lame man which was *immediately* healed held *on to* Peter and John, all *of* the people ran together unto them in *that portion of* the porch that is called Solomon's, greatly wondering *at that which had just happened.*

12.   And when Peter saw *it,* he answered unto *all of* the people *that gathered,* Ye men of Israel, why marvel ye at this *which ye have just seen?* Or why look ye so earnestly on us, as though by our own power or holiness we had made this man to walk?

13.   The *very* God of Abraham, and of Isaac, and of Jacob, the God of our *fore*fathers, hath glorified his *Only Begotten* Son, *the New Creation* Jesus *of Nazareth.* Whom ye delivered up, and *then* denied him in the presence of *Pontius* Pilate, when he *found no guilt in him and* was determined to let *him* go.

14.   But ye denied the Holy One and the Just, and *instead* desired a murderer to be granted unto you.

15.   And killed the Prince of *eternal* life, whom God hath raised *up* from the dead, whereof we are *personal eye* witnesses.

16.   And *it is in* his name, *and* through faith in his name, *that he* hath made this man strong *and well,* whom ye see *here* and know. Yea, the *same* faith which is by him hath given him this perfect soundness *right here* in the presence of you all.

17.   And now, brethren, I wot that *it was* through *spiritual* ignorance *that* ye did *it,* as *did* also your *religious* rulers.

18.   But *all of* those things, which God before had *prophetically* shown by the mouth of all *of* his *anointed* prophets, that *the* Christ should suffer, he hath *now* so fulfilled.

19.   Repent ye therefore *of this grievous sin,* and be converted *unto the truth,* that *all of* your sins may be blotted out, when the times of refreshing shall come from the presence of the Lord.

20.   And he shall *again* send *the New Creation* Jesus Christ *of Nazareth,* which *from* before *his crucifixion* was preached unto you.

21.   Whom the heaven *itself* must receive until the times of *the* restitution of all things *come,* which *our* God hath spoken by the mouth of all *of* his holy prophets since the world began.

22.   For Moses truly said unto the fathers *in the Book of Deuteronomy,* "A Prophet shall the

Lord your God raise up unto you of your brethren, like unto me. *And* him shall ye hear in all things whatsoever he shall say unto you.

23.   And it shall come to pass, *that* every soul *of all of Mankind*, which will not hear that **Prophet**, shall be destroyed from among *all of* the people." *(Deuteronomy 18:15-16)*

24.   Yea, and all *of* the prophets from Samuel and those that follow*ed* after *him*, as many as have spoken, have likewise foretold of these *very* days.

25.   Ye are the children of the prophets, and of the *blood* covenant which God made with our fathers, saying unto Abraham, "And in thy seed shall all the kindreds of the earth be blessed." *(Genesis 12:1-3)*

26.   *Know ye then that* unto you first **God**, having raised up his **Son**, *the New Creation* **Jesus** *from the dead*, *has* sent him to bless you, in turning away every one of you *who will receive it* from his iniquities.

CHAPTER 4

1.   And as they spake *these things* unto the people, the priests, and the captain of the

16

temple *guard*, and the *members of the* Sadducees, came upon them.

2. Being *upset and* grieved that they *had* taught the people, and *had* preached, through *the New Creation* Jesus, the resurrection from the dead.

3. And they laid *their* hands *up*on them, and put *them* in *the* hold*ing cell* unto the next day, for it was now *the* eventide.

4. Howbeit many of them which heard the word *which Peter and John preached,* believed. And the number of the men *that were converted and became Born-Again that day* was about five thousand.

5. And it came to pass on the morrow, that their rulers, and *the* elders, and *the* scribes,

6. And Annas *who was father-in-law to* the high priest, and Caiaphas *who was the high priest that year,* and John *(possibly Johanan Ben Laccai)*, and Alexander *(possibly Alexander Lysimachus)*, and as many as were of the kindred of the high priest, were gathered together at Jerusalem.

7. And when they had set them in the midst *of those that were gathered,* they asked, By what *unnatural* power, or by what *mystical* name, have ye done this *work of healing?*

10

8. Then Peter, filled with the Holy Ghost, said unto them, Ye rulers of the people, and elders of Israel,

9. If we this day be examined of the good deed *which was* done to the impotent man, *and* by what means he is made whole,

10. Be it known unto you all, and to all *of* the people of Israel, that by the name of *the New Creation* Jesus Christ of Nazareth, whom ye *have* crucified, *and* whom *our* God *hath* raised *up* from the dead, *even* by him doth this man stand here before you whole.

11. This *man Jesus* is *indeed* the stone which was set at nought of you builders, which is *now* become the head of the corner.

12. Neither is there salvation *for a man's spirit found* in any other. For there is none other name under *all of* heaven *above,* given among men *on this earth,* whereby we must be saved.

13. Now when they saw the *unusual* boldness of Peter and John, and perceived that they were *not formally schooled but rather were* unlearned and ignorant men, they marvelled. And *they made a notation* that they had been *in association* with Jesus.

4.   While it remained *with you*, was it not thine own *land*? And after it was sold, was it not *with*in thine own power *to keep all of the monies*? Why hast thou conceived this thing *of evil* in thine heart? Thou hast not *just* lied unto men, but *thou hast lied* unto God.

5.   And Ananias hearing *and having* these words *of truth pierce his heart* fell down, and gave up the ghost. And great fear came *up*on all them that heard *about* these things.

6.   And the young men *of the church* arose, *and* wound him up *in a cloth*, and carried *him* out, and buried *him*.

7.   And it was about the space of three hours after *this had happened*, when his wife *Sapphira*, not knowing what was done, came in *to the gathering*.

8.   And *upon her greeting*, Peter answered unto her, Tell me whether ye *and your husband* sold the land for so much? And she said, Yea, for so much.

9.   Then Peter said unto her, How is it that ye *and your husband* have agreed together to tempt the Spirit of the Lord *our God*? Behold, the feet of them which have *just* buried thy husband *because of his lie*, **are** at the door *right now*, and *they* shall carry thee out *to bury as well*.

10.   Then fell she down straightway at his feet, and yielded up the ghost. And the *same* young men came in *right then*, and found her dead *in the like manner of Ananias*, and carrying *her* forth, buried *her* by her husband.

11.   And *a* great fear *of God* came upon all the church, and upon as many as heard *of* these things.

12.   And by the hands of the apostles were many *other* signs and wonders wrought among the people. And they were all with one accord in Solomon's porch *within the temple area.*

13.   And of the rest *of the people* durst no man join himself to them. But *many of* the people magnified them *because of the move of God.*

14.   And believers were the more *being* added to the Lord, multitudes both of men and *of* women.

15.   Insomuch that they brought forth the sick *and infirmed* into the streets, and laid *them* on beds and couches, that at the *very* least the shadow of Peter passing by might overshadow some of them, *and that they might be healed.*

16.   There came also a multitude *of people* out of the cities round about unto

Jerusalem, bringing *their* sick folks, and them which were vexed with unclean spirits, and they were *all* healed, every one *of them*.

17.   Then the high priest *Caiaphas* rose up, and all they that were with him, (which is the *religious* sect of the Sadducees,) and were filled with indignation *because of the people responding to the power of the gospel.*

18.   And *they* laid their hands on the apostles, and put them in*to* the common prison *for to stop their ministering.*

19.   But the *holy* angel of the Lord *came* by night *and* opened *up* the prison doors, and brought them *all* forth, and said *unto them*,

20.   Go, *and* stand and speak in the temple to *all of* the people, all the words of this *new* life.

21.   And when they heard *that*, they entered into the temple *area* early in the morning, and taught *the people*. But *without knowledge of what the holy angel of the Lord had done,* the high priest came, and they that were with him, and called the council together *again*, and all *of* the *members of the* senate of the children of Israel, and sent *un*to the prison to have them brought *forth.*

22. But when the *appointed* officers came, and found them not in the prison *where they were supposed to be*, they returned *to the council*, and told *them*.

23. Saying, the prison truly found we shut *when we got there* with all safety, and the keepers *were there* standing without before the doors, but when we had opened *the doors*, we found no man within.

24. Now when the high priest and the captain of the temple *guard* and the chief priests heard these things *that the officers shared with them*, they doubted of them *and wondered* whereunto this would grow.

25. Then came one *of their followers* and told them, saying Behold, the men whom ye put in*to the* prison are standing *right now* in the temple *area*, and teaching the people.

26. Then went the captain *of the guard* with the officers, and brought them *to the council* without violence. For they feared *what* the people *might do*, lest they should have been stoned.

27. And when they had brought them *in*, they set *them* before the council. And the high priest asked them,

28. Saying, Did not we straitly command you that ye should not teach *any more* in this name? And behold, *even now* ye have filled *all of* Jerusalem with your doctrine, and *seem to* intend to bring this man's blood upon us.

29.   Then Peter and the *other* apostles *with him* answered *with boldness* and said, We ought to obey God rather than men.

30.   The God of our fathers, *whom we all know of,* raised up *the New Creation* Jesus *of Nazareth,* whom ye slew and hanged *u*pon a tree.

31.   Him hath God *highly* exalted with his right hand *to be* a Prince and a Saviour, for to give repentance to *the Nation of* Israel, and forgiveness of sins *to all who will receive it.*

32.   And we are his *personal eye* witnesses of those things *which have happened.* and *so is* also the Holy Ghost, whom God hath given *freely* to *all* them that obey him.

33.   When they heard *that*, they were cut *to the heart with conviction*, and took counsel to slay them.

34.   Then stood there up one *of the members* in the council, *who was* a Pharisee, named Gamaliel, *who also was* a doctor of the law *of Moses, and was* had in reputation among all *of* the people, and *he* commanded to put the apostles forth a little space.

35. And *he* said unto them, Ye men of Israel, *be careful and* take heed to yourselves what ye *may* intend to do as touching these men.

36. For before these days *in the which we now live, there* rose up Theudas, *who was* boasting himself to be somebody. To whom a number of men, about four hundred, joined themselves *to him*. Who *ultimately* was slain. And all *of them*, as many as *had* obeyed him, were scattered, and *the whole movement was* brought to nought.

37. After this man *Theudas, there* rose up Judas of Galilee in the days of the taxing, and drew away much people after him. He also perished. And all *of his followers,* **even** as many as obeyed him, were dispersed.

38. And now I say unto you *brethren,* Refrain from *pursuing* these men, and let them alone. For if the counsel *they follow* or this work *that they do* be *only* of men, it will come to nought.

39. But if it be of God, ye cannot overthrow it *no matter what ye do*, lest haply ye be found even to fight against God *himself.*

40. And to him they agreed *with what he suggested.* And when they had called the apostles *back into the meeting,* and *had physically* beaten *them*, they commanded *them again* that they should not speak in the name of *the New Creation* Jesus *any more*, and let them go.

41. And they departed from the presence of the council, rejoicing that they were counted worthy *enough* to suffer shame for his name*'s sake.*

42. And daily *both* in the temple, and in every house, they ceased not to teach and *to* preach *about the New Creation* Jesus Christ.

CHAPTER 6

1. And in those *early* days, when the number of the disciples was multiplied, there arose a murmuring of the Grecians against the Hebrews, because their widows were *being* neglected in the daily ministration *of food.*

2. Then the twelve *apostles, which included Matthias,* called the multitude of the disciples *together* **unto them,** and said, It is not reason*able* that we should leave the *study of the* word of God, and serve tables *instead.*

3. Wherefore, brethren, look ye out *from* among *yourselves and find* you seven men of

honest report, *who are* full of the Holy Ghost and *of the* wisdom *of God*, whom we may appoint over this business *of food ministration*.

4. But we will *purpose to* give ourselves continually *un*to prayer, and to the ministry of the *teaching of the* word *of God*.

5. And the saying pleased the whole *of the* multitude *of believers*. And *so* they chose Stephen, a man *who was* full of faith and of the Holy Ghost, and Philip, and Prochorus, and Nicanor, and Timon, and Parmenas, and Nicolas a proselyte *out* of Antioch,

6. Whom they set before the apostles. And when they had prayed, *at the direction of the Holy Spirit* they laid *their* hands *up*on them.

7. And the word of God *went forth and* increased. And the number of the disciples *that were added to the Lord* multiplied in Jerusalem greatly. And a great company of the *Jewish* priests *also* were obedient to the faith *and believed*.

8. And Stephen, *being* full of faith and power, did *show* great wonders and miracles among the people *utilizing the gifts of the Holy Spirit of God*.

9.   Then there arose certain *members* of the synagogue, which is called *the synagogue* of the Libertines; and Cyrenians, and Alexandrians, and of them of Clilcia and of Asia, disputing with Stephen *concerning what he taught and did.*

10.   And they were not able *with their natural wisdom* to resist the wisdom *of God* and the *power of the* Spirit by which he spake.

11.   Then they suborned *corrupt* men, which *falsely* said, We have heard him speak blasphemous words against Moses, and *against* God.

12.   And they stirred up the people *who were willing to listen to them,* and the *unconverted Jewish* elders, and the scribes, and *they* came upon *him,* and caught him *in the temple area,* and brought *him* to the *same* council *that had withstood the apostles.*

13.   And *they* set up false witnesses, which *lied and* said, This man ceaseth not to speak blasphemous words against this holy place, and the law *of Moses.*

14.   For we have *personally* heard him say, that this *New Creation* Jesus of Nazareth *whom he preaches* shall destroy this place, and shall change the customs which Moses *originally* delivered *unto* us.

15.   And all *they* that sat in the council, looking steadfastly on him, saw his face as *if* it had been the face of an *holy* angel.

CHAPTER 7

1.   Then said *Caiaphas* the high priest, Are these things *that they testify against you* so?

2.   And he said, Men, brethren, and *spiritual* fathers, hearken. The God of glory *and of all grace* appeared unto our father Abraham, when he was *yet* in Mesopotamia, before he dwelt in Haran,

3.   And said unto him, "Get thee out of thy *own* country, and *move away* from thy kindred, and come into the land which I shall show thee." *(Genesis 12:1)*

4.   Then *in obedience to God* came he out of the land of the Chaldeans, and *first* dwelt in Haran. And from thence, when his father was dead, he removed him*self* into this land, wherein ye *also* now dwell.

5.   And he gave him none inheritance in it *at that time*, no, not *so much as* to set his foot on. Yet he promised that he would *ultimately* give it to him for a possession, and

to his seed after him, when *as yet* he had no child.

6. And God spake *to Abraham* on this wise, That his seed should sojourn in *Egypt, which was to him* a strange land. And that they should bring them into bondage, and entreat **them** *with* evil *for* four hundred years.

7. "And the nation to whom they shall be in bondage will I judge," said God. "And after that *four hundred year sojourn* shall they come forth, and *shall* serve *only* me in this place." *(Genesis 15:13-14 & 21:12)(Exodus 1:1-14:31)*

8. And he gave him the *blood* covenant *and the covenant sign* of circumcision. And so **Abraham** begat Isaac, and circumcised him *on* the eighth day *as he was instructed*. And Isaac **begat** Jacob, and Jacob **begat** the twelve patriarchs.

9. And the patriarchs *were* moved with envy, *and* sold Joseph into Egypt. But God was with him.

10. And delivered him out of all *of* his afflictions, and gave him favour and wisdom in the sight of Pharaoh, *the* king of Egypt. and he made him *the* governor over Egypt and *over* all *of* his house.

11. Now there came a dearth *of famine* over all *of* the land of Egypt and Canaan,

and great affliction *with it*. And our fathers found no sustenance *in Canaan to nourish them*.

12. But when Jacob heard that there was corn *to be had* in Egypt, he sent out our fathers first, *to fetch the corn and bring it back home to Canaan*.

13. And at the second time *when they were sent out* Joseph was made known *un*to his brethren, and Joseph's kindred was *also* made known unto Pharaoh.

14. Then sent Joseph *his brethren back to Canaan*, and called his father Jacob to *come* unto **him**, and all *of* his kindred *as well*; threescore and fifteen souls.

15. So Jacob *left Canaan and* went down into Egypt, and *there he* died, he, and our fathers *when their time came*.

16. And *when they passed, they* were carried over into *the region of* Shechem, and laid in the sepulchre *there* that Abraham *had* bought for a sum of money of the sons of Hamor, *the father* of Shechem.

17. But when the time of the promise *to leave Egypt* drew nigh, which God had sworn *un*to Abraham, the people grew and multiplied *greatly* in Egypt.

18.   U*n*til another king arose *to the throne,* which knew not Joseph *and what he had done to save Egypt.*

19.   The same *king* dealt subtly with our kindred, and evil entreated our fathers, so that they *made them* cast out their young children, to the end *that* they might not live.

20.   *This all happened* in *the* which time *that* Moses was born. And *he* was exceeding fair, and *was* nourished up *with*in his *own* father's house *for* three months.

21.   And when he was cast out *within a basket of reeds into the river Nile,* Pharaoh's daughter took him up, and *received him and* nourished him for her own son.

22.   And *as* Moses was *being raised up, he was* learned in all the wisdom of the Egyptians, and was mighty in words and in deeds.

23.   And when he was *a* full forty years old, it came into his heart *by the Spirit of Grace* to visit his brethren, the children of Israel.

24.   And seeing one *of them* suffer wrong *at the hands of an Egyptian,* he defended *him,* and avenged him that was oppressed, and smote the Egyptian *in the process.*

25.   For he supposed *that* his brethren would have understood how that God, by his hand, would deliver them *because he was*

part of Pharaoh's household. **But they understood not** *as he supposed.*

26.   **And the next day he showed himself unto them as they strove** *among themselves,* **and would have set them at one again, saying, "Sirs, ye are brethren, why do ye** *this* **wrong one to another?"** *(Exodus 2:13)*

27.   **But he that** *was at ought with the Egyptian and now* **did** *strive with and do* **his** *own* **neighbor wrong thrust him away, saying, "Who made thee** *to be* **a ruler and a judge over us?**

28.   **Wilt thou kill me, as thou didst the Egyptian yesterday?"** *(Exodus 2:14)*

29.   **Then fled Moses at this saying,** *and left Egypt* **and was a stranger in the land of Midian, where he** *married a woman named Zipporah and* **begat two sons.**

30.   **And when forty years were** *fully* **expired, there appeared** *un*to **him in the wilderness of mount Sinai an angel of the Lord in a flame of fire** *with*in **a bush.**

31.   **When Moses saw** *it,* **he wondered at the sight. And as he drew near to behold** *it,* **the voice of the Lord came unto him,**

32.   *Saying,* **"I** *am* **the God of thy fathers. The God of Abraham, and the God of Isaac, and the God of Jacob."** *(Exodus 3:6)* **Then**

Moses trembled, and durst not behold *the bush*.

33.   Then said the Lord to him, "Put off thy shoes from *off of* thy feet, for the place where thou standest is holy ground.

34.   I have seen, I have seen the affliction of my people which is in Egypt, and I have heard their groaning, and am *now* come down to deliver them. And now come *Moses, for* I will send thee into Egypt." *(Exodus 3:5-10)*

35.   This *very* Moses whom they refused, saying, Who made thee a ruler and a judge *over us?* The same did God send *to be* a ruler and a deliverer by the *very* hand of the angel which appeared to him in the bush.

36.   He brought them out, after that he had shown *great* wonders and signs in the land of Egypt, and in the Red Sea, and in the wilderness *for* forty years.

37. This is that *same* Moses, which said unto the children of Israel, "A Prophet shall the Lord your God raise up unto you of your brethren, like unto me, *and* him shall ye hear." *(Deuteronomy 18:15)*

38.   This is he, that was in the church in the wilderness, *and that was* with the angel which spake to him in the mount Sinai, and

also **with** our fathers. **Who** received *from this angel* the lively oracles *that he was* to **give** unto us.

39. **To whom our fathers** *stubbornly* **would not obey, but thrust** *him* *away* **from them, and in their hearts turned back again into Egypt.**

40. *They* **saying unto** *Moses' brother* **Aaron, "Make us gods to go before us. For** *as for* **this Moses, which brought us out of the land of Egypt,** *he has gone up into the mount Sinai, and* **we wot not what is become of him."** *(Exodus 32:1)*

41. **And they made** *for themselves* **a** *golden* **calf in those days, and** *even* **offered sacrifice unto the idol, and rejoiced in the works of their own hands.**

42. **Then God turned** *away from them*, **and gave them up to** *go ahead and* **worship the host of heaven. As it is written in the book of the prophets, "O ye house of Israel, have ye offered** *up un*to **me slain beasts and sacrifices** *by the space of* **forty years in the wilderness?**

43. **Yea, ye took up the tabernacle of Moloch, and the star of your god Remphan, figures which ye made** *by your own hands* **to worship them. And** *so,* **I will**

carry you away beyond Babylon." *(Deuteronomy 18:10)*

44. **Our fathers had the** *earthly* **tabernacle of witness in the wilderness, as he had appointed** *while on the mount,* **speaking unto Moses, that he should make it according to the fashion** *of the true tabernacle in heaven* **that he had seen.**

45. **Which also our fathers that came after** *that generation* **brought in***to the promised land* **with Joshua.** *Right* **into the possession of the Gentiles, whom God drave out before the face of our fathers, unto the days of David.**

46. **Who found favour before God, and desired** *himself* **to find** *place for a* **tabernacle for the God of Jacob.**

47. **But Solomon** *his son is the one who ultimately* **built him a house.**

48. **Howbeit the Most High dwelleth not in** *any earthly* **temples made with hands. As saith the prophet,**

49. **"Heaven** *is* **my throne, and** *the* **earth** *is* **my footstool. What** *kind of* **house will ye build me?" saith the Lord: "Or what** *is* **the place of my rest** *upon this earth?*

50. **Hath not my** *own* **hand made all these things?"** *(Isaiah 66:1-2 & I Kings 8:27)*

51. **Ye stiffnecked and uncircumcised in** *your* **heart and ears** *people.* **Ye do always resist**

the *truth that has been given by the* **Holy Ghost. As your fathers** *did in days gone by,* **so** *do ye also.*

52.   **Which of the prophets have not your fathers persecuted? And they have slain them which** *spoke of and* **showed before, of the coming of the Just One. Of whom ye have been now the betrayers and murderers** *thereof.*

53.   **Who have received the law** *of Moses* **by the** *very* **disposition of angels** *from heaven,* **and** *yet* **have not kept** *it.*

54.   **When they heard these things, they were cut** *deeply un*to **the heart, and they gnashed on him with** *their* **teeth.**

55.   **But he, being full of the Holy Ghost, looked up steadfastly into** *the* **heaven, and saw the glory of God, and** *New Creation* **Jesus** *himself* **on the right hand of God.**

56.   **And** *he* **said** *unto the council,* **Behold, I see the heavens opened, and the Son of man standing on the right hand of God.**

57.   **Then** *unable to listen any further* **they cried out with a loud voice, and stopped their ears, and ran** *violently* **upon him with one accord.**

58.   **And** *they* **cast** *him* **out of the city, and** *taking him to the place of execution, they* **stoned** *him.* **And the witnesses** *to his murder* **laid**

down their clothes at a young man's feet, whose name was Saul *of Tarsus*.

59.   And they stoned Stephen *to death as he was* calling upon God, and saying, Lord Jesus, receive my spirit *into thy hands*.

60.   And he kneeled down, and cried with a loud voice, Lord, lay not this sin to their charge. And when he had said this *last utterance*, he fell asleep.

61.   And *young* Saul *of Tarsus* was *much agreeable and* consenting unto his death.

CHAPTER 8

1.   And at that *same* time *of Stephen's challenging of the religious council*, there was a great persecution *that arose* against the church which was at Jerusalem. And *so* they were all scattered abroad throughout the regions of Judea and Samaria, except *for* the apostles.

2.   And devout men carried *the fallen* Stephen *to his burial*, and made a great lamentation over him.

3.   As for *the young* Saul *of Tarsus*, he made *a* havoc of the church, entering into every *believer's* house, and haling *both* men and

women *everywhere,* committed *them* into *the* prison.

4.   Therefore they that were scattered abroad *because of the persecution,* went every where preaching the word *of God.*

5.   Then *the chosen* Philip went down to the city of Samaria *at the leading of the Holy Spirit,* and preached *the resurrected New Creation* Christ unto them.

6.   And the people, with one accord, gave heed unto those things which Philip spake, *both* hearing and seeing the miracles which he did.

7.   For unclean spirits, crying with *a* loud voice, came out of many that were possessed *with them.* And many taken with palsies, and that were lame, were healed.

8.   And there was great joy within that city.

9.   But there was a certain man, called Simon, which before *this* time in the same city *of Samaria had* used sorcery *or magic,* and bewitched *and bedazzled* the people of Samaria, giving out that *he* himself was some great one.

10.   To whom they all gave heed, from the least to the greatest, saying, This man is the great power of God.

11.   And to him they had regard, because

that of *a* long time he had bewitched *and bedazzled* them with sorceries.

12. But when they *of the city* believed Philip preaching the things concerning the kingdom of *the living* God, and the *power in the* name of *the New Creation* Jesus Christ, they *repented and* were baptized *in water*, both men and women.

13. Then Simon himself *upon hearing the incorruptible word of God* believed also. And when he was baptized *in water utilizing the baptism of John*, he continued *in fellowship* with Philip, and wondered, beholding the *genuine* miracles and signs *of the Holy Spirit* which were done.

14. Now when the apostles, *who were not scattered abroad when the persecution arose, but* which were at Jerusalem heard, *through the testimonies,* that Samaria had received the word of God, they sent unto them Peter and John.

15. Who, when they were come down *to the city*, prayed for them, that they might receive the *baptism of the* Holy Ghost.

16.   (For as *of* yet he was fallen upon none of them *within the city*. Only they were baptized *in water* in the name of the Lord Jesus).

17.   Then laid they *their* hands *up*on them *which believed within the city*, and they received the *baptism of the* Holy Ghost, *and spake with other tongues as the Spirit gave them utterance.*

18.   And when Simon *witnessed and* saw that through *the* laying on of the apostles' hands the Holy Ghost was given, *being carnally minded* he offered them money.

19.   Saying, Give *unto* me also this power, that on whomsoever I lay *my* hands, he may receive the *power of the* Holy Ghost.

20.   But Peter *rebuked him and* said unto him, Thy *worthless* money perish with thee, because thou hast *in error* thought that the *free* gift of God *given to whomsoever would believe and receive* may be purchased with money.

21.   Thou hast neither part nor *any* lot in this matter. For *even though thou hast received the free gift of eternal life through the Lord Jesus Christ,* thy heart is not right in the sight of God.

22.   *I charge thee to* repent therefore of this thy wickedness, and pray *unto* God, if perhaps the *evil* thought of thine heart may be forgiven thee.

23.   For I perceive that thou art in the gall of bitterness, and *in* the bond of iniquity *because the Spirit of Truth hath been demonstrated and thy times of deception have been made manifest.*

24.   Then answered Simon, and said *unto Peter, Thou hast well said. Please intercede and* **pray** ye to the Lord for me, that none of these things which ye have spoken *shall* come upon me.

25.   And they, *the apostles,* when they had testified *of the grace of God,* and preached the word of the Lord *in Samaria,* returned to Jerusalem, and *on their way* preached the gospel in many villages of the Samaritans.

26.   And the angel of the Lord spake unto Philip *in a dream,* saying, Arise, and go toward the south unto the way that goeth down from Jerusalem unto Gaza, which is *in the* desert.

27.   And he arose and went. And, behold, a man of Ethiopia, an *trusted* eunuch of great authority under Candace *the* queen of the Ethiopians, who had the charge of all *of* her treasure, and had come to Jerusalem for to worship *the living God,*

28.   Was returning to *Ethiopia,* and *was* sitting in his chariot *and did* read Isaiah the prophet.

29.   Then the *Holy* Spirit said unto Philip, Go near *to him*, and join thyself to this chariot.

30.   And Philip ran thither to *him*, and heard him read *aloud from* the *scroll of the* prophet Isaiah, and said *unto him*, Understandest thou what thou readest?

31.   And he said *unto Philip*, How can I, except some man *who knoweth what the prophet is saying* should guide me? And he desired Philip that he would come up *into the chariot* and sit with him.

32.   The place of the Scripture which he read *from* was this, "He was led as a sheep to the slaughter; and like a lamb dumb before his shearer, so opened he not his mouth:

33.   In his humiliation his judgment was taken away: and who shall declare his generation? For his life is taken from the earth." *(Isaiah 53:7-8)*

34.   And the eunuch answered Philip, and said, I pray thee, of whom speaketh the prophet this *declaration*? Of himself, or of some other man?

35.   Then Philip opened his mouth *under the inspiration of the Holy Spirit*, and began at the same Scripture *that the eunuch was reading*, and preached unto him *the New Creation* **Jesus Christ** *of Nazareth.*

36. And as they went on *their* way, they came unto a certain *river or pool of* water. And the eunuch said *unto Philip,* See, *here is* water, what doth hinder me to be baptized *in the like manner as you have ministered must take place?*

37. And Philip said, If thou believest with all thine heart, thou mayest. And he answered and said, I believe that *the New Creation* **Jesus Christ** is the Son of God.

38. And he commanded the chariot to stand still. And they went down both *of them* into the water. Both Philip and the eunuch *entered into the water,* and he baptized him *with John's baptism of repentance.*

39. And when they were come up out of the water, the *Holy* Spirit of the Lord caught away *and translated* Philip, that the eunuch saw him no more. And he went on his way rejoicing *and praising the God of Israel.*

40. But *as for* Philip, *he* was found *some twenty-five miles away* at *the outskirts of the city of* Azotus. And *so* passing through *the city* he preached *the gospel there, and* in all *of* the cities, *un*til he came to Caesarea.

CHAPTER 9

1.   And *the young* Saul *of Tarsus*, yet breathing out threatening and slaughter against the disciples of the Lord, *because of his zealousness for the traditions of his fathers*, went unto the high priest *of the temple*,

2.   And desired of him letters to *the city of* Damascus *and* to the synagogues *within the city*, *stating* that if he found any *members* of this *new* way, whether they were men or women, he might *arrest them and* bring them bound unto Jerusalem.

3.   And as he journeyed *on his mission*, he came near *unto the city of* Damascus. And suddenly there shined round about him a *brilliant* light from heaven.

4.   And he fell *off of his horse on*to the earth, and heard a voice *speaking and* saying unto him, "Saul, Saul, why persecutes thou me?"

5.   And he said, Who art thou, Lord? And the Lord said, "I am Jesus *of Nazareth* whom thou persecutest, it is hard for thee to kick against the pricks."

6.   And he trembling and astonished said, Lord, what wilt thou have me to do? And the Lord *said* unto him, "Arise, and go

into the city, and it shall be told *unto* thee what thou must do."

7.　And the men *of the posse* which journeyed with him stood *there* speechless, hearing a voice *of conversation coming from young Saul,* but seeing no man *around that he was expressly speaking to.*

8.　And Saul arose from the earth, and when his eyes were *physically* opened *from the brilliance of the light,* he saw no man *for he was now blind.* But they led him by the hand, and brought *him* into *the city of* Damascus.

9.　And he was *there within the city for* three days without sight, and *during that time* neither did *he* eat *any food* nor drink *any liquid.*

10.　And there was a certain disciple *of the Lord* at Damascus, named Ananias. And to him said the Lord in a vision, "Ananias". And he said, Behold, I am here Lord.

11.　And the Lord *said* unto him, "Arise, and go into the street which is called Straight, and inquire in the house of Judas for one called Saul, of Tarsus, for, behold, he prayeth.

12.　And hath seen in a vision a man named Ananias coming in*to the house,* and putting *his* hand *up*on him, that he might receive his sight."

13.   Then Ananias answered, Lord, I have heard *rumors and testimonies* by many *believers,* of this man *and* how much evil he hath done to thy saints at Jerusalem.

14.   And here he hath *received* authority from the chief priests *of the city* to bind *with cords* all that call *up*on thy name.

15.   But the Lord said unto him, "Go thy way. For he is a chosen vessel unto me, *destined* to bear my name before the Gentiles, and *before* kings, and *before* the children of Israel *as well.*

16.   For I will show *unto* him how *many* great things *that* he must suffer for my name's sake."

17.   And Ananias went *on* his way *as instructed,* and entered into the house. And putting his hands *up*on him said, Brother Saul, the Lord, *even the New Creation* Jesus *of Nazareth,* that *hath* appeared unto thee in the way as thou camest, hath *indeed* sent me, that thou mightiest receive thy *physical* sight, and be filled with *the power of* the Holy Ghost *unto salvation.*

18.   And immediately there fell from *off of* his eyes as it had been scales. And he received sight forthwith, and arose and was baptized *in water with John's baptism of repentance.*

19. And when he had received meat *and drink for nourishment*, he was strengthened. *"And, immediately he conferred not with flesh and blood. Neither went he up to Jerusalem to them which were apostles before him, but he went into Arabia, and returned again unto Damascus."* (Galatians 1:16b-17)

19a. Then was Saul certain days with the disciples which were at Damascus.

20. And straightway he preached Christ in the synagogues, that he is the *true* Son of God.

21. But all that heard *him* were amazed *at his behaviour*, and said, Is not this he that destroyed them which called on this name in Jerusalem, and *then indeed* came hither for that *same* intent, that he might *arrest them and* bring them bound *with cords* unto the chief priests?

22. But *the young* Saul increased the more in *knowledge and spiritual* strength, and confounded the *unconverted* Jews which dwelt at Damascus, proving *from the Scriptures* that this *New Creation Jesus* is *the* very Christ.

23. And after that many days were fulfilled, the *unconverted* Jews *through frustration* took counsel *together* to kill him.

24. But their *attempt at* laying await *for him* was known of Saul. And they watched the

51

gates day and night *trying* to *catch him that they might* kill him.

25.   Then the disciples *of the Lord* took him by night, and *let* him down *to the ground* by the wall, in a basket.

26.   And when *the young* Saul was *finally* come to Jerusalem, he assayed to join himself to the disciples *of the Lord.* But they were all afraid of him *because of his reputation,* and believed not that he was *indeed* a disciple of *the New Creation Jesus of Nazareth.*

27.   But Barnabas, *the son of consolation,* took him, and brought *him* to the apostles *Peter and James,* and declared unto them how he had *personally* seen the Lord *Jesus* in the way, and that he had spoken *unto* him *concerning what he had called him to do,* and how he had preached *to the unconverted Jews* boldly at Damascus in the name of *the New Creation* Jesus.

28.   And he was with them *a fortnight of time,* coming in and going out at Jerusalem.

29.   And *while he was there* he spake boldly, *as he had in Damascus,* in the name of the *New Creation* Lord Jesus, and *further* disputed against the Grecians: *that is . . . unconverted Greek-Jews who had lived in areas where the Greek*

language was spoken. **But they** *did not receive him and indeed* **went about to slay him.**

30. **Which when the** *believing* **brethren knew,** *in order to save his life,* **they brought him down to Caesarea, and** *from thence* **sent him forth to** *his hometown, the city of* **Tarsus.**

31. **Then,** *with young Saul in Tarsus,* **had the churches rest** *from their fears* **throughout all** *of* **Judea and Galilee and Samaria, and** *they* **were** *all* **edified. And** *they were* **walking in the fear of the Lord, and in the comfort of the Holy Ghost,** *and they* **were multiplied.**

32. **And it came to pass,** *that* **as Peter passed throughout all** *quarters,* **he came down also to the saints which dwelt at** *the city of* **Lydda.**

33. **And there he found a certain man named Aeneas, which** *being infirmed* **had kept his bed eight years, and was sick of the palsy.**

34. **And Peter said unto him** *under the inspiration of the Holy Spirit,* **Aeneas,** *the New Creation Lord* **Jesus Christ maketh thee whole. Arise, and make thy bed. And he arose immediately.**

35. **And all** *of the people* **that dwelt at Lydda and Sharon,** *and that* **saw him,** *believed* **and turned to the Lord.**

36. Now there was at *the city of* Joppa *at this time* a certain disciple named Tabitha, which by interpretation is called Dorcas. This woman was full of good works and almsdeeds which she did.

37. And it came to pass in those days, that she was *very* sick, and *ultimately* died. Whom when they had washed *her body*, they laid *her on the bed* in an upper chamber.

38. And forasmuch as Lydda was *quite close by and* nigh *un*to Joppa, and *since* the disciples had heard that Peter was there *in Lydda*, they sent unto him two men, desiring *him* that he would not delay to come *un*to them.

39. Then Peter arose and went with them *at their bidding. And* when he was come *to Joppa*, they brought him unto the upper chamber *where Dorcas lay.* And all *of* the widows stood by him *and were* weeping, and showing the coats and garments which Dorcas *had* made, while she was *still* with them.

40. Put Peter put them all forth *from the room*, and kneeled down, and prayed. And *under the inspiration of the Holy Spirit,* turning *him*self to the body *he* said, Tabitha, *I say unto*

thee arise. And she opened *up* her eyes, and when she saw **Peter,** she *smiled and* sat up.

41.   And he *gently* gave her *his* hand, and lifted her up. And when he had called the *weeping* saints and widows, he presented her alive *unto them.*

42.   And it was *something that became* known throughout all *of* **Joppa.** And *because of that* many believed in the *New Creation* **Lord** *Jesus.*

43.   And it came to pass, that he tarried many days *there* in **Joppa** with one *named* **Simon** *who was* a tanner.

CHAPTER 10

1.   There was a certain man in **Caesarea** called **Cornelius,** *who was* a *Roman* centurion of the band *of people* called the Italian *band,*

2.   *He was a* devout *man,* and one that *believed in and* feared *the living* **God** with all *of* his house. Which gave much alms to the *poor* people, and prayed to *the One True* **God** alway*s.*

3.   He saw in a vision evidently, about the ninth hour of the day, an angel of God coming in to him *where he was,* and saying unto him, Cornelius.

4.　　And when he looked on him, he was afraid, and said, What is it, Lord? And he said unto him, Thy prayers and thine alms *gifts* are come up *and presented at the throne* for a memorial before *the living* God.

5.　　And now *I instruct thee to* send men to *the city of* Joppa, and *have them* call for *one* Simon, whose surname is Peter.

6.　　He *now* lodgeth with one Simon *who is* a tanner, whose house is *close* by the sea side. He shall *then* tell thee what thou oughtest to do.

7.　　And when the angel which spake unto Cornelius was departed *from him*, he called two of his household servants, and a devout *Roman* soldier *from among all* of them that waited *up*on him continually.

8.　　And when he had declared all *of* these things unto them, he sent them to Joppa.

9.　　*The next day,* on the morrow, as they went on their journey, and drew nigh unto the city, *Simon* Peter went up upon the housetop to pray about the sixth hour *of the day*.

10.　　And he became very hungry, and would have eaten. But while they made ready *the meal,* he fell into a trance,

11. And *he* saw *the* heaven opened, and a certain vessel descending unto him, as *if* it had been a great sheet *that was* knit *together* at the four corners, and *it was* let down to the earth.

12. Wherein were all manner of fourfooted beasts of the earth, and wild beasts *also*, and creeping things, and fowls of the air.

13. And there came *the sound of* a voice to him, *saying,* "Rise *up*, Peter, kill *from among these beasts*, and eat *them*."

14. But Peter *protested and* said, Not so, Lord, for I have never *broken the law of Moses and* eaten any thing that is common or unclean.

15. And the voice *spake* unto him again the second time *saying,* "What *the Lord* God hath cleansed, that call not thou common."

16. *And* this was done thrice. And *then* the vessel was received up again into heaven.

17. Now while Peter *thought about these things and* doubted *with*in himself what this vision, which he had *just* seen should mean, behold, the *very* men which were sent from Cornelius had *arrived and* made inquiry for *where* Simon's house *was*, and *now* stood before the gate.

18. And *they* called *out*, and asked whether Simon, which was surnamed Peter, were lodged there.

19. While Peter *continued to give* thought on the vision, the *Holy* Spirit said unto him, "Behold, *there are* three men *that* seek thee.

20. Arise therefore, and get thee down, and go *away* with them, doubting nothing, for I have sent them *to you*."

21. Then Peter went down to the men *that were waiting* which were sent unto him from Cornelius, and said, Behold, I am he whom ye seek. What is the cause wherefore ye are come *here*?

22. And they said, Cornelius the *Roman* centurion, *who is* a just man, and one that feareth *the true living* God, and *is* of *a* good report among all *of* the nation of the Jews, was *recently* warned from God by a holy angel to send for thee, *to come* into his house, and *when ye come*, to hear words of thee.

23. Then called he them in*to the house*, and lodged *them* *overnight*. And on the morrow Peter went away with them, and certain *Born-Again* brethren from Joppa accompanied him.

24. And *on* the *next* morrow after, they entered into *the city of* Caesarea. And

Cornelius *had* waited for them *to come*, and had called together *all of* his kinsmen and near friends.

25.　And as Peter was coming in*to the house*, Cornelius met him, and fell down at his feet, and worshipped *him*.

26.　But Peter *restrained him and* took him up, saying, Stand up, I myself also am a man.

27.　And as he talked with him, he went in, and found many that were come together.

28.　And he said unto them, Ye know how that it is an unlawful thing for a man that is a Jew to keep company, or come unto one of another nation. But God *himself* hath shown me that I should not call any *other* man common or unclean.

29.　Therefore, *because of that,* came I *unto you* without *any* gainsaying, as soon as I was sent for. I ask *you now* therefore for what intent ye have sent for me?

30.　And Cornelius said, Four days ago I was fasting until this *very* hour. And at the ninth hour I prayed *with*in my house, and behold, a *holy angel that looked like a* man stood before me in bright clothing,

31. And said *unto me*, Cornelius, thy prayer is heard, and thine alms *gifts* are had in remembrance in the sight of God.

32. Send therefore *un*to Joppa, and call hither *for one* Simon, whose surname is Peter. He is lodged in the house of *one* Simon *who is* a tanner *living* by the sea side. Who, when he cometh *to thee*, shall speak unto thee *words of life*.

33. Immediately therefore I sent *un*to thee. And *I perceive* thou hast well done that thou art come. Now therefore are we all *gathered* here, present before God, to hear all *of the* things that are commanded thee of God.

34. Then Peter opened *his* mouth, *and began to speak* and said, Of a truth I perceive that God *indeed* is no respecter of persons.

35. But in every nation *on earth* he that feareth him, and worketh righteousness, is accepted with him.

36. The word which *God* sent unto the children of Israel, *is the* preaching *of* peace by Jesus Christ *of Nazareth*. He is *the* Lord of all.

37. That *same* word, *I say*, ye know. *That* which was published throughout all *of*

Judea, and began from Galilee, *soon* after the baptism which John preached.

38. How *that* God *in heaven* anointed Jesus of Nazareth *his Son* with the Holy Ghost and with power. Who went about doing good, and healing all that were oppressed of the devil, for God was with him.

39. And we are witnesses of all *of the* things which he did, both in the land of the Jews, and in *the city of* Jerusalem. Whom they slew and hanged *up*on a tree *because of their jealousy and hatred.*

40. Him God raised up *on* the third day, and showed him openly.

41. Not to all *of* the people, but unto *only select* witnesses chosen before of God, *even* to us *his apostles,* who did eat and drink with him after he rose from the dead.

42. And he *is the one who* commanded us to preach unto *all of* the people, and to testify that it is he which was ordained of God *to be* the Judge of *the* quick and the dead.

43. To him give all *of* the *holy* prophets witness, that through his name, whosoever believeth in him shall receive *the* remission of *his* sins.

44. While Peter yet spake these words, *the people gathered with Cornelius believed in their hearts*

unto righteousness and the Holy Ghost fell on all *of* them which heard the word.

45. And they of the circumcision *background* which *now* believed, *and had come with him,* were astonished, as many as came with Peter. Because that on the *pagan, heathen,* Gentiles also was *now* poured out the gift of the Holy Ghost *even as Jesus had promised.*

46. For they *of the circumcision background* heard them *begin to* speak with *other* tongues, and magnify God. Then answered Peter *and said,*

47. Can any man *here* forbid water, that these *which have believed* should not be baptized? *They also are them* which have received the Holy Ghost as well as we.

48. And he commanded them to be baptized *with John's baptism of repentance* in the name of the Lord *Jesus.* Then prayed they him to *stay with them a while and to* tarry certain days.

CHAPTER 11

1. And the apostles and *the believing* brethren that were in Judaea heard that the Gentiles had also received the word of God *and the baptism of the Holy Ghost.*

2. And when Peter *returned and* was come up to Jerusalem, they that were of the *believing* circumcision contended with him,

3. Saying *unto him,* Thou wentest in to men *who were* uncircumcised, and *ye* didst eat with them.

4. But Peter *had* rehearsed *the matter* from the beginning, and expounded *it* by order unto them *who protested,* saying,

5. *Only a short while ago* I was in the city of Joppa praying. And in a trance I saw a vision *of* a certain vessel *which did* descend, *looking like* as it had been a great sheet, let down from heaven by *the* four corners, and it came even *un*to me.

6. Upon the which when I had fastened mine eyes, I considered *what I was looking at,* and saw fourfooted beasts of the earth, and wild beasts *also,* and creeping things, and fowls of the air.

7. And I heard *the sound of* a voice saying unto me, "Arise, Peter. Slay *from among these beasts* and eat *them.*"

8. But I said, Not so, Lord. For nothing common or unclean hath at any time entered into my mouth, *as it is commanded within the law of Moses.*

9. But the voice answered *unto* me again from *the* heaven, "What God hath cleansed, *that* call not thou common."

10. And this was done three times. And *then they* all were drawn up again into *the* heaven.

11. And, behold, immediately there were three men already come unto the house *of Simon* where I was, *who had been* sent from Caesarea unto me.

12. And the *Holy* Spirit *within me* bade me go with them, nothing doubting. Moreover, these six *believing* brethren accompanied me *on my journey*, and we entered into the man's house.

13. And he showed *unto* us how he had seen an angel in his house, which stood and said unto him, Send men to Joppa and call for Simon, whose surname is Peter.

14. Who *when he comes* shall tell *unto* thee words, whereby thou and all *of* thy house shall be saved.

15. And as I began to speak, *they believed the word of the Lord within their hearts, and* the Holy Ghost fell *up*on them, as *he had* on us at the beginning.

16. Then remembered I the word of the Lord *Jesus*, how that he said, "John indeed

baptized *thee* with water, but ye shall be baptized with the Holy Ghost *not many days hence.*" *(Joel 2:28)(Acts 1:5)*

17.   Forasmuch then as God *himself* gave them the like gift as *he did* unto us, who believed on the Lord Jesus Christ, what was I, *to think* that I could withstand God?

18.   *And* when they heard these things, they held their peace, and glorified *the living* God, saying, Then hath God also to the Gentiles *graciously* granted repentance unto *everlasting* life.

19.   Now they which were scattered abroad upon the persecution that arose about Stephen, *had* travelled as far as Phoenicia, and Cyprus, and Antioch, preaching the word *of the Lord* to none *other* but unto the Jews only.

20.   And some of them were *the* men of Cyprus and Cyrene, which, when they were come *un*to Antioch, spake unto the Grecians, *and were* preaching the *resurrected New Creation* Lord Jesus.

21.   And the hand of the Lord was with them. And a great number *of them* believed, and turned unto the Lord.

22.   Then *the* tidings of these things came unto the ears of the church which was in

Jerusalem. And they sent forth Barnabas, that he should go as far as Antioch *to check it out.*

23.   Who, when he came *hither,* and had seen the *manifested* grace of God, was glad, and exhorted them all, that with purpose of heart they would cleave unto the Lord.

24.   For he was a good man, and *was* full of the Holy Ghost and of faith. *And because of his influence* much people was added unto the Lord.

25.   Then departed Barnabas to *the city of* Tarsus, for to seek Saul *who had returned unto his hometown some thirteen years earlier, at the direction of the Lord Jesus himself, and because of death threats.*

26.   And when he had found him, he *persuaded him and* brought him *back* unto Antioch *with him.* And it came to pass, that *for* a whole year they assembled themselves *together* with the church, and taught much people. And the disciples *of the Lord* were called *Christians* first in Antioch.

27.   And *also* in these days came prophets *of the Lord* from Jerusalem unto Antioch.

28.   And there stood up one of them *in the church* named Agabus, and signified by *a gift of* the *Holy* Spirit that there should be *coming a*

great dearth throughout all the *known* world.
Which came to pass *with*in the days of
Claudius Caesar.

29.   Then the disciples, every *single* man
according to his *own financial* ability,
determined to send relief unto the brethren
which dwelt in Judea.

30.   Which also they did, and sent it to the
elders *of the church at Jerusalem* by the hands of
Barnabas and Saul.

CHAPTER 12

1.   Now about that *same* time Herod the
king stretched forth *his* hands to vex certain
members of the church.

2.   And he killed James, *the son of Zebedee,*
the brother of John with the sword.

3.   And because he saw *that* it pleased the
unconverted Jews, he proceeded further to take
Peter also *into custody.* (Then were the days of
the Feast of Unleavened Bread.)

4.   And when he had apprehended him,
he put *him* in*to the local* prison, and delivered
him in*to the hands of* four quaternions of
soldiers *in order* to keep him. *He* intending
after Easter to bring him forth to the people
for trial.

5. Peter therefore was kept in *the* prison. But prayer was made without ceasing of the *members of the* church, unto God for him.

6. And when *the time came that* Herod would have brought him forth, the same night, Peter was sleeping between two soldiers. *He was* bound with two chains, and the keepers *that were* before the door kept the prison *guarded.*

7. And, behold, the angel of the Lord came upon *him*, and a light shined *with*in the prison. And he smote Peter on the side, and raised him up, saying *unto him*, Arise up quickly! And his chains fell off from *his* hands.

8. And the angel said unto him, Gird thyself, and bind on thy sandals. And so he did. And he saith unto him, Cast thy garment about thee, and follow me.

9. And he went out *of the cell*, and followed him. And *he* wist not that it was *really* true which was done by the angel, but *rather* thought *that* he saw a vision.

10. When they *both* were past the first and the second ward, they came unto the *main* iron gate that leadeth unto the city, which opened *up un*to them of his own accord. And they went out, and passed on through one street, and *suddenly* forthwith the angel departed from him.

11.   And when Peter was come to himself, he said, Now I know of a surety, that the Lord hath sent his angel *to help me*, and hath delivered me out of the hand of Herod, and *from* all *of* the expectation of the people *which had been gathered* of the Jews.

12.   And when he had *pondered and* considered *the thing*, he came to the house of Mary the mother of John, whose surname was Mark, where many *believers* were gathered together praying.

13.   And as Peter knocked at the door of the gate, a damsel came to hearken *unto the knock, who was* named Rhoda.

14.   And when she *had heard him, and* knew *that it was* Peter's voice, she opened not the gate for *the* gladness *within her*, but ran in *to where the others were*, and told *them* how *that* Peter stood *outside*, before the gate.

15.   And they said unto her, Thou art mad. But she constantly affirmed that it was even so *as she had said*. Then said they, It is his angel *that thou hast heard*.

16.   But Peter continued knocking. And when they *finally* had opened *the door*, and *really* saw him, they were astonished.

17.   But he, beckoning unto them with the hand *and motioning unto them* to hold their peace, declared unto them how the Lord had brought him out of the prison *by his angel.* And he said, Go *now, and* show these things unto James, *Jesus' half-brother, who was the head of the church,* and to the brethren. And *then* he departed, and went into another place.

18.   Now as soon as it was day, there was no small stir among the soldiers, *as to* what was become of Peter.

19.   And when Herod *desired and* had sought for him, and found him not *in the prison,* he examined the keepers, and *because Peter was found missing,* he commanded *them* that *they* should be put to death. And he *himself* went down from Judaea *un*to Caesarea, and *there he* abode.

20.   And Herod was highly displeased with them of Tyre and Sidon. But they came with one accord to him *anyway,* and having made Blastus the king's chamberlain their friend, *they* desired peace. Because their country was nourished by the king's *country.*

21.   And upon a set day Herod, arrayed in royal apparel, sat upon his throne, and made an oration unto them.

22.   And the people *responded and* gave a shout, *saying,* **It is** the voice of a god *that we hear,* and not of a man.

23.   And *because Herod did not rebuke the people for their declaration,* immediately the angel of the Lord smote him, because he gave not God the glory. And *within a short period of time* he was eaten *up* of worms, and gave up the ghost.

24.   But the word of God *continued, and* grew and multiplied.

25.   And Barnabas and Saul returned from Jerusalem *to Antioch,* when they had fulfilled *their* ministry, and took *back* with them John, whose surname was Mark.

CHAPTER 13

1.   Now there were in the church that was at Antioch certain prophets and teachers, *such* as Barnabas, and Simeon that was called Niger, and Lucius of Cyrene, and Manaen, which had been brought up with Herod the Tetrarch, and *also* Saul *of Tarsus.*

ACTS 13:2

2   As they ministered to the Lord, and fasted, the Holy Ghost said *unto them*, Separate *unto* me Barnabas and Saul for the work whereunto I have called them.

3.   And when they had fasted *further* and prayed *for guidance*, and laid *their* hands on them, they sent *them* away.

4.   So they, being sent forth by the *direction of the* Holy Ghost, departed *from Antioch* unto *the seaport city of* Seleucia *in Syria*. And from thence they *took ship and* sailed *un*to *the island of* Cyprus.

5.   And when they were at *the city of* Salamis, they preached the word of God in the synagogues of the Jews. And they had also John *Mark* to *assist in their* ministering.

6.   And when they had gone through the isle unto *the city of* Paphos, they found a certain *spiritual* sorcerer, a false prophet, a Jew, whose name *was* Barjesus.

7.   Which was *in association* with the deputy of the country, Sergius Paulus, *who himself was* a prudent man, who called for Barnabas and Saul, and desired to hear the word of God.

8.   But Elymas the sorcerer (for so is his name by interpretation) withstood them *in*

what they preached, seeking to turn away the deputy from the faith.

9.   Then Saul, (who *from now on* also *is going to be* **called** Paul), filled with the *power of the* Holy Ghost, set his eyes *up*on him,

10.   And said *by the direction and gifting of the Holy Spirit*, O full of all subtilty and all mischief, *thou* child of the devil *himself*, *thou* *stated* enemy of all righteousness, wilt thou not cease to pervert the right ways of the Lord *God Almighty?*

11.   And now, behold, the hand of the Lord is upon thee, and thou shalt be blind. Not *capable of* seeing the sun for a season. And immediately there fell on him a mist and a darkness. And he *could not see and* went about seeking some*one* to lead him by the hand.

12.   Then the deputy, *Sergius Paulus,* when he saw what was done, believed *the word of God*, being astonished at the doctrine of the Lord.

13.   Now when Paul and his company loosed from Paphos, they came to *the city of* Perga in *the region of* Pamphylia. And John *Mark* departing from them *suddenly,* returned *un*to Jerusalem.

14.   But when they departed from Perga, they came to *the city of* Antioch in *the region of* Pisidia, and *again* went into the *Jewish* synagogue on the sabbath day *of commandment*, and sat down.

15.   And after the *normal* reading of the law and *of* the prophets, the rulers of the synagogue sent unto them, saying, *Ye* men *and* brethren, if ye have any word of exhortation for the people, say on.

16.   Then Paul stood up, and beckoning with *his* hand *boldly* said, Men of Israel, and ye that fear *the living* God, give audience.

17.   The God of this people of Israel chose our fathers, and exalted the people when they dwelt as strangers in the land of Egypt. And with a high arm *of mighty signs and wonders* brought he them out of it *after many years of bondage.*

18.   And about the time of forty years suffered he their manners *of bad behaviour* in the wilderness.

19.   And when he had destroyed seven *different* nations in the land of Canaan, he divided their *promised* land to them by lot.

20.   And after that, he *graciously* gave **unto them** judges *for* about the space of four

hundred and fifty years, until *the time of* Samuel the prophet.

21. And afterward they *were not satisfied with Samuel and* desired *for God to give them* a king. And God gave unto them Saul the son of Kish, a man *who was* of the tribe of Benjamin, by the space of forty *more* years.

22. And when he had removed him *because of his disobedience*, he raised up unto them David to be their king. To whom also he gave *a* testimony, and said: "I have found *in* David, *the son* of Jesse, a man after mine own heart, which shall fulfill all my will."
(Psalms 89:29)

23. Of this man's seed hath God, according to *his* promise, raised *up* unto Israel a Saviour, *who is* Jesus *Christ of Nazareth*:

24. When John had first preached, before his coming, the baptism of repentance to *prepare the hearts of* all the people of Israel.

25. And as John *had* fulfilled his course, he said, Whom think ye that I am? *For* I am not *he*. But, behold, there cometh one after me, whose shoes *latchet* of *his* feet I am not worthy to loose.

26. Men *and* brethren, children of the stock of Abraham *our father*, and whosoever

that among you feareth **God,** to you is the word of this salvation *that I speak of* **sent.**

27.   For they that dwell at **Jerusalem,** and their rulers, because they *spiritually* **knew him not, nor yet the voices of the prophets which are read every sabbath day, they have** *virtually* **fulfilled** *them* **in condemning** *him.*

28.   And *even* **though they found no cause of death** *in him,* **yet desired they** *Pontius* **Pilate that he should be slain.**

29.   And when they had fulfilled all that was written of him, they took *him* **down from the tree, and laid** *him* **in a sepulchre.**

30.   But **God raised him** *up* **from the dead** *as a New Creature.*

31.   And he was seen many days of them which came up with him from **Galilee** to **Jerusalem,** who are his witnesses unto the people.

32.   And *now* **we declare unto you** *the* **glad tidings, how that the promise which was made unto the fathers,**

33.   **God hath fulfilled the** *very* **same unto us their children, in that he hath raised up Jesus** *Christ of Nazareth* **again** *to be a New Creature. Even* **as it is also** *prophetically* **written in the second psalm, "Thou art my Son, this day have I begotten thee."** *(Psalms 2:7)*

34. And as concerning *the fact* that he raised him up from the dead, *now* no more to return *un*to corruption, he said on this wise, "I will give *unto* you the sure mercies of David." *(Psalms 18:50 & 89:3-4 & 89:20-24 & 89:35-37; Isaiah 55:3)*

35. Wherefore he *prophetically* saith also in *yet* another *psalm*, "Thou shalt not suffer thine Holy One to see corruption." *(Psalms 16:10)*

36. For David, after he had served his own generation by the will of God, fell on sleep, and was laid unto his fathers, and *indeed* saw corruption.

37. But he, whom God *hath* raised *up* again, saw no corruption.

38. Be it known unto you therefore, men *and* brethren, that through this man, *the New Creation Jesus* is preached unto you the forgiveness of *your* sins.

39. And by him, all that *choose to* believe are justified from all things, from which ye could not be justified by the law of Moses.

40. Beware therefore, lest that come upon you, which is spoken of in the prophets, *in the book of Habakkuk*; "Behold, ye despisers, and wonder, and perish. For I *will* work a work in your days, a work which ye shall in no wise believe, *even* though a man declare it unto you." *(Habakkuk 1:5)*

41. And when the Jews were gone out of the synagogue, the Gentiles *which had been outside and listening to what Paul was preaching,* besought that these words might be preached *un*to them the next sabbath.

42. Now when the congregation was broken up, many of the Jews and religious proselytes followed Paul and Barnabas. Who, speaking to them, persuaded them to continue in the grace of God.

43. And the next sabbath day came almost the whole city together to hear the word of God.

44. But when the *unconverted* Jews saw the multitudes, they *became jealous and* were filled with envy *because the word of God was received by the Gentiles,* and spake against those things which were spoken by Paul, contradicting and blaspheming.

45. Then Paul and Barnabas waxed bold *again,* and said, It was necessary that the word of God should first have been spoken *un*to you. But seeing *that* ye put it from you, and judge yourselves unworthy of everlasting life, lo, we *will* turn *now* to the Gentiles.

46. For so hath the Lord commanded us, *saying,* "I have set thee to be a light of the

Gentiles, that thou shouldest be for salvation unto the ends of the earth." *(Isaiah 49:6)*
47. And when the Gentiles heard this, they were glad, and glorified the word of the Lord. And as many as were ordained *of God before the world began un*to eternal life, believed.
48. And the word of the Lord was published throughout all the region.
49. But the *unbelieving* Jews stirred up the devout and honorable women, and the chief men of the city, and raised persecution against Paul and Barnabas, and expelled them out of their coasts.
50. But they shook off the dust *from off* of their feet against them, and came unto Iconium.
51. And the disciples were filled with joy, and with the *power of the* Holy Ghost.

CHAPTER 14

1. And it came to pass *with*in *the city of* Iconium, that they went both together into the synagogue of the Jews *again, as was their custom,* and so spake *the word of the Lord. The result being* that a great multitude both of the Jews and also of the Greeks believed.

2.   But the unbelieving Jews *wickedly*
stirred up the Gentiles, and made their
minds evil affected against the *believing*
brethren.

3.   *For a* long time therefore abode they *in
Iconium* speaking boldly in the *name of the New
Creation* Lord, which gave testimony unto
the word of his grace *as he promised*, and
granted signs and wonders to be done by
their hands.

4.   But the *great* multitude of the city was
divided. And part *of them* held with the
unbelieving Jews, and *the other* part *of them* with
the apostles.

5.   And when there was an assault made
upon them both of the Gentiles, and also of
the Jews, with their rulers, *they sought* to use
them despitefully, and *ultimately* to stone
them.

6.   *And when* they were *made a*ware of *it,
they* fled unto Lystra and Derbe, *which were*
cities of Lycaonia, and unto the region that
lieth round about *them*.

7.   And there they *were safe, and* preached
the gospel *without any hindrance*.

8.   And there sat a certain man at Lystra,
who was impotent in his feet, being a cripple

from his mother's womb, who never had walked.

9.	The same *man* heard Paul speak, who steadfastly beholding him, and perceiving *by the gifting of the Holy Spirit* that he had faith to be healed,

10.	Said with a loud voice *unto him*, Stand upright on thy feet. And *obeying Paul's command* he leaped *up* and walked.

11.	And when the people saw what Paul, *by the Holy Spirit,* had done, they lifted up their voices, saying in the speech of Lycaonia, The gods are come down to us in the likeness of men.

12.	And they called Barnabas, Jupiter, and Paul, Mercurius, because he was the chief speaker.

13.	Then the priest of *the Roman god* Jupiter, which was *a leader* before their city, brought oxen and garlands unto the gates, and would have done *a* sacrifice with *all of* the people.

14.	*Which* when the apostles, Barnabas and Paul, heard *of,* they rent their clothes, and ran in among the people, crying out *with a loud voice,*

15.	And saying, Sirs, *we beseech thee,* why do ye these things? We also are *just* men, of like passions *along* with you. And *we do* preach unto you that ye should turn *yourselves* from these vanities unto the living God. *He* which made *the* heaven and the earth, and the sea, and all *of the* things that are therein.

16.   Who in times past suffered *and endured* all nations to walk in their own ways.

17.   Nevertheless he left not himself without *a* witness, in that he *always* did good, and gave us *the* rain from heaven, and fruitful *plenteous* seasons, filling our *bellies and our* hearts with food and gladness.

18.   And with these sayings scarce restrained they the people, *so* that they had not done *their intended* sacrifice unto them.

19.   And, *in time,* there came thither *certain of the wicked* Jews from Antioch *in Pisidia* and Iconium, who *spoke evil of the apostles and* persuaded the people *to kill them.* And, having stoned Paul, *they* drew *him* out of the city, supposing *that* he had been dead.

20.   Howbeit, as the disciples *gathered together and* stood round about him, *they fervently prayed and* he rose up, and came *right back* into the city. And *then* the next day, he departed with Barnabas *and went on* to Derbe.

21.   And when they had preached the gospel *in the synagogue* to that city, and had taught many *receptive Jews and Gentiles*, they *retraced their steps and* returned again to Lystra, and *to* Iconium, and *back again to* Antioch.

22.   Confirming the souls of the *new* disciples, *and* exhorting them to continue in the faith, and *teaching them* that we must through much tribulation enter into the kingdom of God.

23.   And when they had ordained *unto* them elders in every church *that had been established*, and had prayed with fasting, they commended them *into the hands of* the Lord, on whom they believed.

24.   And after they had *again* passed throughout *all of the province of* Pisidia, they came to Pamphylia.

25.   And when they had *once again* preached the word in *the city of* Perga, they went down into *the region of* Attalia.

26.   And *from* thence *they* sailed *back* to Antioch, from whence they had been recommended to the grace of God for the work which they *had* fulfilled. *And in so doing, had completed their first missionary journey.*

27.   And when they were come, and had gathered *all of* the church together, they

rehearsed all that God had done with them, and how he had opened the door of faith unto the Gentiles.

28. And there they abode, *at Antioch, for a* long time with the *other* disciples.

CHAPTER 15

1. And *in time,* certain *Judaizing* men which came down from Judaea taught the brethren, **and said,** except ye be circumcised after the manner of *the law of* Moses, ye cannot be saved. *"And Peter was at Antioch at that time, and he dissembled himself from the Gentile believers because of what these men taught, and his dissimulation even affected Barnabas."* (Galatians 2:11-13)

2. When therefore Paul and Barnabas had no small dissension and disputation with them, they determined that Paul and Barnabas, and certain other of them, should go up to Jerusalem unto the apostles and elders *that were there* about this question, *and they sought to settle this issue.*

3. And being brought on their way by the church, they passed through *the regions of* Phoenicia and Samaria, declaring *as they went*

the conversion of the Gentiles. And *with that
news* they caused great joy unto all *of* the
brethren.

4. And when they were come to
Jerusalem, they were *graciously* received of
the church, and *of* the *other* apostles and
elders, and they declared all *of the* things
that God had done with *and through* them.

5. But there rose up certain of the sect of
the Pharisees which believed, saying *just as
the Judaizers did*, that it was needful to
circumcise them, and to command *them* to
keep the law of Moses.

6. And the apostles *of the Lord* and *the*
elders came together for to consider *the
ramifications* of this matter.

7. And when there had been much
disputing *from various individuals*, Peter rose
up, *having repented of his fearful behavior in Antioch*,
and said unto them, Men *and* brethren, ye
know how that a good while ago, *when I
abode in Joppa*, God made choice among us,
and sent us to the Roman centurion Cornelius' house,
that the Gentiles, by my *very own* mouth,
should hear the word of the gospel, and
believe.

8.   And God, which knoweth the hearts *of all men*, bare them witness. Giving *unto* them the *baptism of the* Holy Ghost, even as *he did* unto us *at the beginning.*

9.   And *in so doing, hath* put no difference between us and them, purifying their hearts *as well* by faith.

10.   Now therefore, why tempt ye *the living* God, *by trying* to put a yoke *of bondage* upon the neck of the *new Gentile* disciples, which neither our fathers *before us,* nor we, were able to bear?

11.   But we believe that through the grace of the *New Creation* Lord Jesus Christ we shall *all* be saved, *if we believe,* even as they *have experienced.*

12.   Then all *of* the *gathered* multitude kept silence, and gave audience to Barnabas and Paul. Declaring what miracles and wonders God had wrought among the Gentiles by them *as they went forth at the direction of the Holy Ghost.*

13.   And after they *all had finished speaking their minds, and* had held their peace, James, *who was the half-brother of the Lord Jesus,* answered saying, Men *and* brethren, hearken unto me.

14.   Simeon hath declared how *that* God at the first did visit the Gentiles, to take out of them a people for his name.

15.   And to this *demonstration of the Holy Ghost* agree the words of the prophets. As it is written *by Amos*,

16.   "After this I will return, and will build again the tabernacle of David, which is fallen down. And I will build again the ruins thereof, and I will set it up.

17.   That the residue of *Jewish* men might seek after the Lord, and all *of* the Gentiles, upon whom my name is called, saith the Lord *God Almighty*, who doeth all these things." *(Amos 9:11-12)*

18.   Known unto God are all *of* his works from the *very* beginning of the world.

19.   Wherefore my sentence is, that we trouble not them *with the keeping of the law of Moses*, which from among the Gentiles are turned to God.

20.   But that we write unto them *to exhort them*, that they abstain from *the* pollution of idols, and **from** *committing* fornication, and **from** *eating* things *that have been* strangled, and **from** *the eating of* blood *which has been designed by God to carry the force of life.*

21.   For Moses of old time hath in every city them that preach him, being read in the synagogues every sabbath day.

22.   Then pleased it *both* the apostles and elders, with the whole church *at Jerusalem*, to send chosen men of their own company to Antioch, *along* with Paul and Barnabas. *So they chose* Judas *who was* surnamed Barsabas, and Silas, *both of which were* chief men among the brethren.

23.   And they wrote *letters* by them after this manner: The apostles and elders and brethren *of the church of Jerusalem* send greeting unto the brethren which are of the Gentiles, in Antioch and Syria and Cilicia.

24.   Forasmuch as we have heard, that certain *of them* which went out from us have troubled you with words, subverting your souls, saying, *Ye must* needs be circumcised and keep the law *of Moses.* To whom we gave no *such* commandment.

25.   It seemed good unto us, being assembled with one accord *to deal with this issue,* to *officially* send chosen men unto you, *along* with our beloved Barnabas and Paul.

26.   Men that have hazarded their *very* lives for the name of our *New Creation* Lord Jesus Christ.

27. We have sent therefore Judas and Silas, who shall also tell *you* the same things by *their very own* mouth.

28. For it seemed good to the Holy Ghost, and to us, to lay upon you no greater burden than these necessary things:

29. That ye abstain from meats offered *un*to idols, and from *the eating of* blood *which has been designed by God to carry the force of life*, and from *the eating of* things *that have been* strangled, and from *committing* fornication. From which if ye *obey what we have decreed and* keep yourselves, ye shall do well. Fare ye well.

30. So when they were dismissed, they came to Antioch. And when they had gathered the multitude together, they delivered the epistle.

31. **Which** when they had read *what was sent*, they rejoiced for the consolation.

32. And Judas and Silas, being prophets also themselves, exhorted the brethren *in Antioch* with many words, and confirmed **them** *in the Holy Ghost.*

33. And after they had tarried *there for* a space *of time*, they were let go in peace from the brethren *to return unto Jerusalem and* unto the apostles.

34. Notwithstanding it pleased Silas to abide there still *in Antioch*.

35. Paul also and Barnabas continued *ministering* in Antioch, *both* teaching and preaching the word of the Lord, *along* with many others also.

36. And some days after *this*, Paul said unto Barnabas, Let us go again and visit our *newly converted* brethren in every city where we have *before* preached the word of the Lord, *and see* how they do.

37. And Barnabas *was* determined to take with them John, whose surname was Mark.

38. But Paul thought *it* not good to take him with them, who *had* departed from them from Pamphylia *without cause*, and went not with them to the work *that the Holy Spirit sent them to do*.

39. And the contention was so sharp between them *over this issue*, that they departed asunder one from the other. And so, Barnabas took Mark, and *at his discretion* sailed unto Cyprus.

40. And Paul chose Silas *as a ministering partner*, and departed, being recommended by the brethren unto the grace of God.

41. And he *and Silas* went through Syria and Cilicia *by land*, confirming the churches.

CHAPTER 16

1. Then came he to *the cities of* **Derbe** and **Lystra**. **And, behold, a certain disciple was there, named Timothy, the son of a certain woman, which was a Jewess, and** *she* **believed** *in the Lord Jesus Christ*. **But his father was a** *Gentile* **Greek.**

2. *He was a good man* **which was well reported of by the brethren that were at** *the cities of* **Lystra and Iconium.**

3. *Timothy impressed Paul, and he felt that he would be an asset to the ministerial team. So,* **him would Paul have to go forth with him. And** *he* **took and circumcised him** *according to the law of Moses,* **because of the Jews which were in those quarters. For they knew all that his father was a** *Gentile* **Greek,** *and Paul desired that nothing be left undone that might hinder the ministry.*

4. **And as they went through the cities** *within the region of Galatia,* **they delivered** *to* **them the decrees, that were ordained of the apostles and** *the* **elders which** *attended the meeting and* **were** *part of the church* **at Jerusalem.**

5. **And so were the churches** *where Paul, Silas, and Timothy ministered,* **established in the faith, and increased in** *their* **number daily.**

6. Now when they had gone throughout Phrygia and the *entire* region of Galatia, and *then* were forbidden of the Holy Ghost to preach the word *of the Lord* in Asia, *they rested.*

7. After, *when* they were come to *the province of* Mysia, they assayed to go into *the province of* Bithynia. But the *Holy* Spirit suffered them not *to go.*

8. And *so, when* they *were* passing by Mysia, *they* came down to *the city of* Troas.

9. And a vision appeared to Paul in the *middle of the* night. *In the vision* there stood a man of Macedonia, and prayed him, saying, Come over into Macedonia, and help us.

10. And after he had seen the vision, immediately we endeavoured to go into Macedonia, assuredly gathering that the Lord *Jesus* had called us for to preach the gospel unto them.

11. Therefore loosing from Troas, we came with a straight course to *the island of* Samothracia, and the next *day came un*to *the seaport city of* Neapolis.

12. And from thence *we came* to Philippi, which is the chief city of that part of Macedonia, **and** a *Roman* colony. And we

were in that city abiding *a* certain *number of* days.

13.   And on the sabbath *we could not locate a synagogue, so* we went out of the city *and down* by a river side, where prayer was wont to be made *by the Jewish women of the city*, and we sat down, and spake unto the women which resorted *thither.*

14.   And a certain woman named Lydia, *who was* a seller of purple *fabrics*, of the city of Thyatira, which worshipped *the One True* God, heard *us, as we spoke.* Whose heart the Lord opened *unto us*, that she attended unto the things which were spoken of *by* Paul.

15.   And when she was *water* baptized, and her *whole* household, she besought *us*, saying, If ye have judged me to be faithful to the Lord, come into my house, and abide *there.* And she constrained us.

16.   And it came to pass, *that* as we went to prayer, a certain damsel *which was* possessed with a spirit of divination met us, which *had* brought her masters much gain by soothsaying.

17.   The same *woman* followed Paul and us, and cried *out*, saying, These men are the servants of the most high God, which *will* show unto us the way of salvation.

18. And this did she many days *in a row*. But *at a point in time* **Paul,** being grieved *with her behaviour,* turned and said *un*to the *foul* **spirit,** *under the inspiration of the Holy Spirit,* **I** command thee in the name of *the New Creation* **Jesus Christ** *of Nazareth* to come out of her. And he came out the *very* same hour.

19. And when her masters saw that the hope of their gains was gone *because she could no longer tell fortunes,* they caught **Paul** and **Silas,** and drew *them* into the market place, unto *where the* **rulers** *of the city gather,*

20. And brought them *un*to the magistrates, saying, These men, being **Jews** *from afar,* do exceedingly trouble our city.

21. And *they* teach customs, which are not lawful for us to receive, neither *for us* to observe, being *that we are* **Romans.**

22. And the multitude *that had observed these things* rose up together against them. And the magistrates rent off their clothes, and commanded *for* to beat *them.*

23. And when they had laid many stripes upon them, they cast *them* into the prison *without a trial,* charging the jailer to keep them safely.

24. Who, having received such a charge, thrust them into the inner*most part of the*

prison, and made their feet fast in the stocks.

25. And at midnight Paul and Silas prayed, and sang praises unto God. And *all of* the *other* prisoners heard them.

26. And suddenly there was a great earthquake. So *great* that the *very* foundations of the prison were shaken. And immediately all *of* the doors *of the prison cells* were opened, and every one's bands were loosed.

27. And the keeper of the prison, *as he was* awakening out of his sleep, and *now* seeing *all of* the prison doors open, drew out his sword, and would have killed himself, supposing that *all of* the prisoners *would have seized the opportunity, and* had been fled.

28. But *before the jailer could use his sword* Paul cried *out* with a loud voice, saying, Do thyself no harm, for *none of us have fled and* we are all *still* here.

29. Then he called *his associate* for a light, and sprang in*to the prison cell area,* and came trembling, and fell down before Paul and Silas.

30. And *he* brought them out *of the prison,* and said, Sirs, what must I do to be saved *and receive the joy that I have heard you sing about?*

31. And they said *unto him*, Believe on the *New Creation* Lord Jesus Christ, and thou shalt be saved, and *so shall* thy *whole* house *if they do likewise.*

32. And they spake unto him the word of the Lord, and *preached* to all that were in his house.

33. And he took them *to his house* the same hour of the night, and washed *their* stripes. And *he* was *water* baptized, he and all his *house*, straightway.

34. And when he had brought them into his house, he set meat before them, and rejoiced *with them*, believing in God with all *the members of* his house.

35. And when it was day, the magistrates sent the sergeants *unto the jailer*, saying, Let those men go.

36. And the keeper of the prison told this saying to Paul, The magistrates *of the city* have sent to let you go. Now therefore, depart and go in peace.

37. But Paul said unto them, They have beaten us openly *and* uncondemned, *we* being Romans. And have *further*, cast *us* into prison. And now do they *attempt* to thrust us out privily? Nay verily, but let them come themselves *personally* and fetch us out.

38.   And the sergeants told these words unto the magistrates. And they feared *greatly* when they heard that they were Romans.

39.   And they came *personally* and besought them, and brought *them* out, and *desired them* to depart out of the city.

40.   And they went out of the prison, and entered *again* into *the house of* Lydia. And when they had seen the brethren, they comforted them, and *then* departed.

CHAPTER 17

1.   Now when they had passed through *the cities of* Amphipolis and Appolonia, they came to *the city of* Thessalonica, where *there* was a synagogue of the Jews.

2.   And Paul, as his manner was, went in unto them, and *for* three sabbath days reasoned with them out of the Scriptures.

3.   Opening and alleging, that *the* Christ must needs have suffered, and *died, and be* risen again from the dead. And that this *New Creation* Jesus, whom I preach unto you, is *indeed the* Christ.

4.   And some of them believed, and consorted *further* with Paul and Silas. And of

the devout **Greeks** *there was* a **great multitude. And of the chief women** *of the city,* *there was* **not a few.**

5.   **But the Jews which believed not,** *were* **moved with envy,** *and* **took unto them***selves* **certain lewd fellows of the baser sort, and gathered a** *whole* **company, and set all** *of* **the city on an uproar. And** *they* **assaulted the house of Jason, and sought to bring them out to** *all of* **the** *angry* **people.**

6.   **And when they found them not** *in the house,* **they drew Jason and certain** *other* **brethren unto the rulers of the city, crying, These that have turned the** *whole* **world upside down** *with their doctrine* **are come hither also,**

7.   **Whom Jason hath** *willingly* **received. And these all do contrary to the decrees of Caesar, saying that there is another king** *to be worshipped,* **one** *New Creation* **Jesus** *Christ.*

8.   **And they troubled the people and the rulers of the city, when they heard these things.**

9.   **And when they had** *extorted and* **taken security of Jason, and of the others, they let them go.**

10.   **And the** *faithful* **brethren immediately sent away Paul and Silas by night unto**

Berea, who coming *thither* went into the synagogue of the Jews.

11.	These *individuals* were more noble than those in Thessalonica, in that they received the word *of God* with all readiness of mind, and searched the Scriptures daily, whether *or not* those things *which they heard preached* were so.

12.	Therefore many of them believed *the word of the Lord.* And, also of *the* honorable women *of the city* which were Greeks, and of *the* men, not a few.

13.	But when the *wicked* Jews of Thessalonica had knowledge that the word of God was *being* preached of Paul at Berea, they came thither also *without delay*, and stirred up the people.

14.	And then immediately the brethren sent away Paul to go, as it were, to the sea. But Silas and Timothy abode there still *at Berea.*

15.	And *so,* they that conducted Paul *forth*, brought him unto Athens. And receiving a commandment *from Paul, to give* unto Silas and Timothy for to come *un*to him with all speed, they departed *and returned unto Berea.*

16.	Now while Paul waited for them at Athens, his spirit was stirred in him, when he saw *that* the city *was* wholly given *over un*to idolatry.

17. Therefore disputed he in the synagogue with the Jews, and with the devout persons *of the city*, and in the market *place, on a* daily *basis* with them that met with him.

18. Then certain philosophers of the Epicureans, and of the Stoics, encountered him. And some *of them* said, What will this babbler *have to* say? Other some *said*, He seemeth to be a setter forth of strange *new* gods. *And these things they said* because he preached unto them *New Creation* Jesus, and the resurrection *from the dead.*

19. And *so* they took him, and brought him unto Areopagus, saying *unto him*, May we know what this new doctrine *is*, whereof thou speakest?

20. For thou bringest certain strange things to our ears. We would *want to* know therefore what these things mean.

21. (For all *of* the Athenians, and strangers which were there, spent *all of* their time in nothing else, but either to tell or to hear *tell of* some new thing.)

22. Then Paul stood *up* in the midst of Mar's hill, and said, *Ye* men of Athens, I

perceive that in all things ye are *indeed much* too superstitious.

23. For as I passed by, and beheld your devotions, I found an altar with this inscription: **TO THE UNKNOWN GOD.** Whom therefore ye ignorantly worship, him declare I unto you.

24. God that made the world, and all *of the* things therein, seeing that he is *the* Lord of *the* heaven and *of the* earth, dwelleth not in *any* temples made with hands.

25. Neither is *he* worshipped with *aught of* men's hands, as though he needed any thing. Seeing *that* he *it is that* giveth to all *things their* life, and breath, and all *other* things.

26. And hath made of one blood, all *of the* nations of men for to dwell on all the face of the earth. And hath determined the times before appointed, and the bounds of their habitation.

27. That they should seek the Lord, if haply they might feel after him, and find him, though he be not far from every one of us.

28. For *it is* in him *that* we live, and move, and have our being. As certain also of your own poets have said, "For we are also his off-spring."

29. Forasmuch then as we are the offspring of God, we ought not to think that the Godhead is like unto gold, or silver, or stone, *that is* graven by art and man's device.

30. And the times of this ignorance God *has* winked at *in the past*, but now commandeth all men every where to repent.

31. Because he hath appointed a *certain* day, in the which he will judge the world in righteousness by *that* man whom he hath ordained. *Whereof* he hath given assurance *of that* unto all *men*, in that he hath raised him from the dead.

32. And when they heard of the resurrection of the dead, some *of them* mocked. And others said, We will hear *of* thee again of this *matter.*

33. So Paul departed from among them.

34. Howbeit certain men clave unto him, and believed *right away.* Among the which was Dionysius the Areopagite, and a woman named Damaris, and *certain* others with them.

CHAPTER 18

1. After these things Paul departed from Athens, and came *un*to *the city of* Corinth.

2. And found a certain Jew named Aquila, *who was* born in Pontus, *but* lately come from Italy, with his wife Priscilla, (because that Claudius *Caesar* had commanded *that* all *of the* Jews *were to* depart from *out of* Rome,) and *he* came unto them.

3. And because he was of the same craft, he abode with them, and wrought *his works.* For by their occupation, they were tentmakers.

4. And he reasoned *with*in the synagogue every sabbath *of commandment,* and persuaded *both* the Jews and the Greeks.

5. And when Silas and Timothy *finally* were come from Macedonia, Paul was pressed in the spirit, and testified to the Jews *that New Creation* Jesus *of Nazareth* **was** Christ.

6. And when they *became upset and* opposed themselves, and blasphemed, he shook *his* raiment, and said unto them, Your blood be upon your own heads, I *am* clean. From henceforth I will go unto the Gentiles.

7.   And he departed thence, and entered into a certain *man's* house, *who was* named Justus. *He was **one*** that worshipped God, whose house joined hard *and was right next door* to the synagogue.

8.   And Crispus, the chief ruler of the synagogue, *also* believed on the Lord with all *of* his house. And many of the Corinthians hearing *the word of the Lord* believed, and were *water* baptized.

9.   Then spake the Lord *un*to Paul in the night by a vision, *and said,* "Be not afraid, but speak, and hold not thy peace.

10.   For I am with thee, and no man shall set on thee to hurt thee, for I have much people in this city."

11.   And he continued *there,* *in Corinth,* a year and six months, teaching the word of God among them.

12.   And *at the time* when Gallio was the *Roman* deputy of *the region of* Achaia, the Jews made insurrection with one accord against Paul, and brought him to the judgment seat,

13.   Saying, This *fellow* persuadeth men to worship God contrary to the law *of Moses.*

14.   And when Paul was now about to open *his* mouth *in defense of the allegations,*

Gallio said unto the Jews, If it were a matter of wrong *doing* or *of* wicked lewdness, O *ye* Jews, reason would *have it* that I should bear with you.

15. But if it be a question of words and names *concerning your religion*, and *of* your law *of Moses*, look ye *to it*, for I will be no judge of such *matters.*

16. And he drave them from the judgment seat.

17. Then all *of* the Greeks took Sosthenes *the Jew*, *who was* the chief ruler of the synagogue, and beat *him up right* before the judgment seat. And Gallio *was not moved, and* cared for none of those things.

18. And Paul after *this* tarried *there in Corinth* yet a good while, and then took his leave of the brethren, and sailed thence into Syria. And *he took* with him Priscilla and Aquila, having shorn *his* head in *the city of* Cenchrea, for he had *made* a vow.

19. And *on his way* he came to Ephesus, and left them there. But he himself entered into the synagogue, *as was his custom*, and reasoned with the Jews.

20. When they desired *him* to tarry *a* longer time with them, he consented not.

21.   But *rather* bade them farewell, saying, I must by all means keep this Feast *of Passover* that cometh in Jerusalem. But I *declare that I* will return again unto you, if God will *have me to come.* And he sailed *away* from Ephesus.

22.   And when he had landed at Caesarea, and gone up, and saluted the church *there*, he went down to Antioch *having completed his second missionary journey.*

23.   And after he had spent some time *in Antioch*, he departed, and went *back* over *all* the country of Galatia and Phrygia in *the* order *that they had gone before*, strengthening all *of* the disciples.

24.   And a certain Jew named Apollos, born at Alexandria *in Egypt*, *who was* an eloquent man, *and* mighty in the Scriptures, came to Ephesus.

25.   This man was instructed in the way of the Lord. And being fervent in the spirit, he spake and taught diligently the things of the Lord, knowing only *of* the baptism *of repentance that was* of John.

26.   And he began to speak boldly in the *Jewish* synagogue. Whom, when Aquila and Priscilla had heard *speak*, they took him unto *them*selves and expounded unto him the way of God more perfectly.

27.   And when he was disposed to pass into Achaia, the brethren wrote *a letter*, exhorting the disciples *there* to receive him *in Christ*. Who, when he was come, helped them much which had believed through grace.

28.   For he mightily convinced the Jews publicly *concerning the gospel*, showing, by the Scriptures, that *New Creation* Jesus was *indeed the* Christ.

CHAPTER 19

1.   And it came to pass, that, while Apollos was at Corinth, Paul having passed through the upper coasts *of the country* came to Ephesus. And finding certain disciples,

2.   He said unto them, Have ye received the Holy Ghost since ye *first* believed? And they said unto him, We have not so much as *even* heard whether there be any Holy Ghost.

3.   And he said unto them, Unto what then were ye *originally* baptized? And they said, Unto John's baptism.

4.   Then said Paul, John verily baptized with the baptism of repentance *in preparation*

of the coming of the Messiah, saying unto the people, that they should believe on him which should come after him, that is, on Christ Jesus.

5. When they heard *this,* they were baptized *in water again,* in the name of the Lord Jesus, *as he had commanded.*

6. And when Paul had laid *his* hands upon them, the Holy Ghost came on them, and they spake with *other* tongues, and prophesied.

7. And all *of* the men were about twelve *in number.*

8. And he went into the synagogue, and spake boldly for the space of three months *concerning the revelations that he had received from the New Creation Lord Jesus.* Disputing *with them about the law of Moses* and persuading *them from the writings of the prophets on* the things *prophetically declared* concerning the kingdom of God.

9. But when divers *of the Judaizers* were hardened *in their heart,* and believed not, but *rather* spake evil of that *New* Way before the multitude, he departed from them, and separated the *new* disciples *of the Lord from the synagogue, and began* disputing daily *with*in the school of one *named* Tyrannus.

10. And this *he* continued by the space of two *whole* years. So, that *which came to pass, was that* all they which dwelt in Asia heard the word of the *New Creation* Lord Jesus, both *the* Jews and *the* Greeks.

11. And *during this time,* God *the Holy Spirit* wrought special miracles by the hands of Paul.

12. So that from *contact with* his *own physical* body were brought unto the sick *many* handkerchiefs or aprons. And the diseases departed from them *by the power of God,* and the evil spirits *living within* went out of them.

13. Then certain of the vagabond Jews, *who were practicing* exorcists, took *it* upon them*selves* to call *out* over them which had evil spirits, the name of the Lord Jesus, saying, We adjure you by Jesus whom Paul preacheth.

14. And there were seven sons of *one named* Sceva, *who was* a Jew, **and** *was the* chief of the priests, which did so *attempt to use the name of Jesus.*

15. And the evil spirit *which possessed the man* answered *unto them* and said, Jesus I know, and Paul I know, but who are ye?

16. And the man in whom the evil spirit was *living,* leaped *up*on them, and overcame

them, and prevailed against them. So that they *all* fled out of the house *stripped* naked *of their clothing* and *physically* wounded.

17.   And this was *something that became* known to all *of* the Jews, and *to the* Greeks also *who were* dwelling at Ephesus. And fear fell on them all, and the name of the *New Creation* Lord Jesus was magnified.

18.   And many that believed *in the Lord* came, and confessed *their errors*, and *openly* showed their deeds.

19.   Many of them also which used curious arts brought their *occult* books together, and burned them *openly* before all **men**. And *when* they counted the price of them, and *totaled the sum, they* found *it to be* fifty thousand *pieces* of silver.

20.   So mightily grew the word of God and prevailed.

21.   After these things were ended, Paul *left Ephesus and* purposed in the spirit, when he had passed through Macedonia and Achaia, to go *un*to Jerusalem, saying, After I have been there, I must also see Rome.

22.   So he sent *back* into Macedonia *again* two of them that *had* ministered unto him, Timothy and Erastus. But he himself stayed in Asia for *another* season.

23.   And *at* the same time there arose no small stir about that *New* **Way** *of following the New Creation Jesus of Nazareth.*

24.   **For** *there was* a certain *man* named **Demetrius,** a silversmith, which *had* made silver shrines for *the false goddess* **Diana,** *and had* brought no small gain unto the craftsmen *of the city.*

25.   *Of* whom *when* he called *them all* together, with *other of* the workmen of like occupation, *addressed them* and said, Sirs, ye know *how* that by this craft we have *all amassed* our wealth.

26.   Moreover ye see and hear, that not alone at **Ephesus** *only,* but almost throughout all *of* **Asia,** this **Paul** hath persuaded and turned away much people, saying that they be no gods, which are made with hands.

27.   So that not only this our craft is in danger to be set at nought, but also that the temple of the great goddess **Diana** *herself* should be despised; and her magnificence should be destroyed, *of* whom all *of* Asia and the *known* world worshippeth.

28.   And when they heard *these sayings,* they were full of wrath, and cried out *with*

one voice, saying, Great *is* Diana of the Ephesians.

29. **And** *because of the anger of the idol makers, that was stirred toward Paul and his ministration of the word of God,* **the whole city was filled with confusion.** *Unable to find and arrest Paul,* **and having caught Gaius and Aristarchus, men of Macedonia,** *being* **Paul's companions in travel, they rushed with one accord into the** *open-air* **theatre** *within the city.*

30. **And when** *word reached* **Paul** *concerning what had happened, he* **would have entered in***to the theatre to speak* **unto the people,** *but* **the disciples suffered him not** *to go in.*

31. **And certain of the chief** *men* **of Asia, which were his friends, sent** *word* **unto him, desiring** *him* **that he would not adventure himself** *into harm's way by going* **into the theatre.**

32. **Some** *of the people* **therefore cried one thing, and some** *of the others cried* **another. For the assembly was confused, and the more part** *of them* **knew not wherefore they were** *even* **come together.**

33. **And** *so* **they drew Alexander out of the multitude, the** *ardent* **Jews putting him forward. And Alexander beckoned with the hand, and would have** *calmed the multitude and* **made his defense unto the people.**

34. But when they knew that he *himself* was a Jew, all *the more*, with one voice, about the space of two hours *they* cried out, Great *is the goddess* Diana of the Ephesians.

35. And when the townclerk had appeased *and settled* the people, he said, *Ye* men of Ephesus, what man is there *among you* that knoweth not how that the city of the Ephesians is a worshipper of the great goddess Diana, and of the *image of her* which fell down from Jupiter?

36. Seeing then that these things cannot be spoken against, ye ought to be quiet, and *purpose* to do nothing rashly.

37. For ye have brought hither *before us* these men, which are neither robbers of churches, nor yet blasphemers of your goddess.

38. Wherefore if Demetrius, and the craftsmen which are *in league* with him, have a *legal* matter against any man, the law is open *and available*, and there are deputies *standing by, so* let them implead one another.

39. But if ye inquire any thing *further* concerning other matters, it shall be determined in a lawful assembly.

40. For *right now* we are in danger to be called in*to* question *by Rome* for this day's

uproar. *Legally speaking* there being no cause whereby we may *justify and* give an account of this concourse.

41.   And when he had thus spoken *to all of the people*, he dismissed the assembly.

CHAPTER 20

1.   And after the uproar was ceased, Paul called unto *him* the disciples *of the Lord*, and embraced *them*, and *then* departed for to go into Macedonia.

2.   And when he had gone over those parts, and had given *unto* them much exhortation, he came into Greece,

3.   And abode *there* with *the believers for* three months. And when the *unbelieving* Jews laid *in* wait for him *to arrest him* as he was about to sail into Syria, he purposed to return *unto Antioch by going back* through Macedonia.

4.   And there *were men who* accompanied him into Asia. Sopater of Berea; and of the Thessalonians, Aristarchus and Secundus. And Gaius of Derbe, and Timothy, and of *the men of* Asia, Tychicus and Trophimus.

5.   These *all taking journey and* going *on*

before, tarried for us at Troas.

6. And we sailed away from *the Roman colony of* Philippi after the *feast* days of Unleavened Bread. And *we* came unto them to Troas in five days *time*, where we abode *with them for an additional* seven days.

7. And upon *Sunday,* the first *day* of the week, when the disciples came together to break bread, Paul preached unto them, *being* ready to depart *from them* on the morrow, and continued *in* his speech until midnight.

8. And there were many lights *burning* in the upper chamber, *and it became quite warm* where they were gathered together.

9. And there sat in a window a certain young man named Eutychus, being fallen into a deep sleep *because of the warmth.* And as Paul was long *winded in his* preaching, he *had* sunk down with *heavy* sleep, and *suddenly* fell down from the third *floor* loft, and was taken up dead.

10. And Paul, *moved with compassion, and at the direction of the Holy Spirit,* went down, and fell *up*on him, and embracing *him* said, Trouble not yourselves, for his life is *now* in him.

11. When he therefore was come up again, *after Eutychus had revived,* and had broken bread *with the disciples,* and *then* eaten,

he continued and talked *for* a long while, even *un*til *the* break of day. *And* so, *concluding his time with them,* he departed.

12.   And they brought the young man *Eutychus, who was still alive, into their midst* and were not a little comforted.

13.   And we went *on* before *Paul* to *the* ship, and sailed unto Assos, there intending to take in Paul. For so had he appointed *us to do,* minding himself to go *on by himself* afoot.

14.   And when he met with us at Assos, we *then* took him in*to the ship,* and came *next* to Mitylene.

15.   And we sailed *from* thence, and came the *very* next ***day*** over against *the island of* Chios. And the next ***day*** *after that* we arrived at *the island of* Samos, and tarried *a few hours* at *the city of* Trogyllium. And *setting sail from there,* the next ***day*** we *finally* came to *the seaport city of* Miletus.

16.   For Paul had determined *within himself* to sail *right* by Ephesus, because he would not *want to* spend the time *remaining* in Asia. For he hasted, if it were *at all* possible for him to be at Jerusalem *on* the *Feast* day of Pentecost.

17.   And from Miletus he sent *emissaries* to Ephesus, and called *for* the elders of the

church.

18.   And when they were come *un*to him, he said unto them, Ye know, from the *very* first day that I came into Asia, after what manner *that* I have *behaved myself, having now* been with you at all seasons.

19. Serving the *New Creation* Lord *Jesus* with all humility of mind, and *weeping* with many tears, and *enduring various* temptations, which befell me by the lying in wait of the Jews *that hate me.*

20.   *And* ye know how I kept back nothing that was profitable *unto you,* but have shown you, and have taught you publicly, and *have even gone* from house to house,

21.   Testifying both to the Jews, and also to the Greeks, repentance toward God, and faith toward our *New Creation* Lord Jesus Christ.

22.   And now, behold, I go bound, *not with chains, but* in the spirit unto Jerusalem, not *really* knowing the things that shall befall me there.

23.   Sav*ing* that the Holy Ghost witnesseth *to me* in every city *that I visit,* saying that bonds and afflictions *shall* abide me.

24.   But *I will allow* none of these things *to deter nor* move me. Neither count I my *own*

life dear unto myself, so that I might finish my course *on this earth* with joy. And *complete* the ministry which I have received of the Lord Jesus, to testify *of* the gospel and of the grace of God.

25.   And now, behold, I know *in my spirit* that ye all, among whom I have gone preaching the kingdom of God, shall see my face no more.

26.   Wherefore I take you to record this day, that I *am* pure, *and free,* from the blood of all *men.*

27.   For I have not shunned *my responsibility* to declare unto you all *of* the counsel of God.

28.   Take heed therefore unto yourselves, and to all the flock, over the which the Holy Ghost hath made you overseers, to feed the church of God, which he hath purchased with his own blood.

29.   For I know this *by the Holy Spirit* , that after my departing shall grievous *religious* wolves enter in among you, not sparing the flock.

30.   Also, *even* of your own selves shall men arise, speaking perverse things, to draw away disciples after them*selves.*

31.   Therefore *be diligent to* watch, and remember, that by the space of three years

I ceased not, *at every opportunity,* to warn *each and* every one *of you* night and day with tears.

32.   And now, brethren, I commend you *un*to God, and to the word of his grace, which is able to build you up, and to give you an inheritance among all *of* them which are sanctified *by the Holy Ghost.*

33.   I have coveted no man's silver, or gold, or apparel.

34.   Yea, ye yourselves know that these hands have ministered unto my *own* necessities, and to them that were with me.

35.   I have shown you all things. *And* how that so labouring, ye ought to support the weak, and to remember the words of the Lord Jesus, how he said, "It is more blessed to give than to receive."

36.   And when he had thus spoken *these things,* he kneeled down, and prayed with them all.

37.   And they all wept sore, and fell on Paul's neck, and kissed him.

38.   Sorrowing most of all for the words which he spake, that they should see his face no more. And they accompanied him unto the ship.

CHAPTER 21

1. And it came to pass, that after we *had separated and* were gotten from them, and *the ship* had launched, we came with a straight course unto *the island of* Coos, and the *day* following unto *the isle of* Rhodes, and from thence unto *the seaport city of* Patara.

2. And finding a ship *there that was* sailing over unto Phenicia, we *bought passage and* went aboard, and set forth.

3. Now when we had discovered *the island of* Cyprus, we left it on the left hand *side*, and sailed *directly* into Syria, and landed at *the seaport city of* Tyre. For *it was* there *that* the ship was to unlade her burden.

4. And finding disciples *of the Lord in Tyre*, we tarried there *for* seven days. *Disciples* who said to Paul *once again* through the *Holy* Spirit, that he should not go up to Jerusalem.

5. And when we had accomplished *our visitation within* those days, we departed and went *on* our way. And they all *accompanied us and* brought us on our way, with *their* wives and children, *un*til *we were* out of the city. And we *all* kneeled down on the *sea*shore, and prayed.

6. And when we had *finally* taken our leave one of another, we took *to another* ship, and they returned home again.

7. And when we had finished *our* course *and launched* from Tyre, we came to *the seaport city of* Ptolemais, and *there* saluted the brethren, and abode with them *for* one day.

8. And the next *day*, we that were of Paul's company departed, and *we* came unto *the seaport city of* Caesarea, *and into our own country. In so doing, we completed the third missionary journey.* And *leaving the ship behind* we *went into the city and* entered into the house of Philip the evangelist, which was *one* of the seven *that were chosen to have hands laid upon them.* And we abode with him.

9. And the same man had four daughters, *all* virgins, which did prophesy *under the gifting of the Holy Spirit.*

10. And as we tarried *there for* many days, there came down from Judaea a certain prophet *of the Lord*, named Agabus.

11. And when he was come *in* unto us, *under the direction of the Holy Spirit* he took Paul's girdle *from off of the peg*, and bound his own hands and feet, and said, Thus saith the Holy Ghost, So shall the *unbelieving* Jews at Jerusalem bind the man that owneth this

girdle, and shall deliver *him* into the hands of the Gentiles.

12.   And when we heard these things, both we *of Paul's company*, and they of that place, besought him *greatly* not to go up to Jerusalem.

13.   Then Paul answered, What mean ye to weep and break mine heart? For I am *now* ready not to be bound only, but also to die *if necessary* at Jerusalem for the name of the Lord Jesus.

14.   And when he would not be persuaded, we ceased *from our petitions*, saying, The will of the Lord be done.

15.   And after those days we took up our carriages, and went *on* up to Jerusalem.

16.   There went with us also *certain* of the disciples of Caesarea, and brought with them one Mnason of Cyprus, *who was* an old disciple, with whom we should lodge.

17.   And when we were come to Jerusalem, the brethren received us *very* gladly.

18.   And the *day* following Paul went in with us unto James, *the half-brother of the Lord Jesus, who was the head of the church at Jerusalem.* And all the elders were present *with him*.

19.   And when he had saluted them, he declared particularly what *marvelous* things God had wrought among the Gentiles by his ministry.

20.   And when they *all* heard *it*, they glorified the Lord, and said unto him, Thou seest brother *Paul*, how many thousands of Jews there are which believe *in the New Creation Lord Jesus*. And *yet* they are all *still* zealous of the law *of Moses*.

21.   And they are informed of thee, that thou teachest all the *other* Jews which are among the Gentiles to forsake Moses, saying that they ought not to circumcise *their* children, neither to walk after *all of* the customs *of the law of Moses, and of the feasts of the Lord, and of the sabbaths.*

22.   What is it therefore *that is to be done*? The multitude must *surely* needs come together. For they will hear that thou art come *hither*.

23.   *For your own safety* do therefore this that we *suggest and* say *un*to thee. We have *even now* four men which have a vow on them.

24.   Them take, and purify thyself with them, and be at charges with them, that *you and* they may shave *your* heads. And all *those that come together* may know that those things,

whereof they were informed concerning thee, are *really* nothing. But *let it be seen* **that** thou thyself also walkest orderly, and keepest the law *of Moses.*

25. As touching the Gentiles which believe *in the Lord*, we have written *a decree* **and** concluded, *as ye know,* that they observe no such thing, save only that they keep themselves from *things* offered *un*to idols, and from *eating* blood, and from *things* strangled, and from *committing* fornication.

26. Then Paul, *willing to be all things to all men,* took the *four* men, and the next day purifying himself with them, entered into the temple, to signify the accomplishment of the days of purification, until that an offering should be offered for every one of them *according to Jewish customs and the law of Moses.*

27. And when the seven days were almost ended, the *unbelieving* Jews which were of Asia, *which had heard and knew what Paul preached,* when they saw him in the temple, stirred up all the people, and laid hands on him.

28. Crying out *in a loud voice*, Men of Israel, help *us*! This is the man, that teacheth all *men* every where against the *Jewish* people, and the law *of Moses*, and *against* this place.

And further *hath* brought **Greeks** also into the temple, and hath polluted this holy place.

29. (For they had seen before *this*, *walking* with him in the city, *brother* **Trophimus** *who was* an Ephesian, whom they supposed that Paul had brought into the temple.)

30. And all the city was moved *by this commotion*, and the people ran together, and they took Paul, and drew him out of the temple, and forthwith the doors were shut.

31. And as they went about to kill him, the tidings *of these things* came unto the chief captain of the *Roman* band *Claudius Lysias*, that all Jerusalem was in an uproar.

32. Who immediately took soldiers and centurions, and ran down unto them. And when they saw the *Roman* chief captain and the soldiers, they left *off the* beating of Paul.

33. Then the chief captain came near *unto Paul*, and took him, and commanded *him* to be bound with two chains. And *he* demanded *to know of the people* who he was, and what he had done.

34. And some *of the people* cried one thing, *and* some another, among the multitude. And when he could not know the certainty *of their actions*, for the tumult *that was made*, he

commanded him to be carried into the castle.

35.   And when he came upon the stairs, so it was, that he was borne *aloft* of the soldiers for the violence of the people.

36.   For the multitude of the people *that* followed after, *were* crying, Away with him!

37.   And as Paul was *about* to be led into the castle, he said unto the chief captain, May I speak unto thee? Who *upon hearing the question* said, Canst thou speak Greek?

38.   Art not thou that Egyptian, which before these days madest an uproar, and leddest out into the wilderness four thousand men that were murderers?

39.   But Paul said *unto him, no I am not,* I am a man *which am* a Jew of Tarsus, *a city* in Cilicia, a citizen of no mean *or unruly* city. And, I beseech thee, *please* suffer me to speak unto the people.

40.   And when he had given him license, Paul stood on the stairs, and beckoned with the hand unto *all of* the people. And when there was made a great silence, he spake unto *them* in the Hebrew tongue, saying,

CHAPTER 22

1.   Men, brethren, and fathers, hear ye my defense *which I make* now unto you.

2.   And when they heard that he spake in the Hebrew tongue to them, they kept the more silence. And he saith,

3.   I am verily a man *which am* a Jew *like unto yourselves*, born in Tarsus, *a city* in Cilicia, *and* yet *raised and* brought up in this city *studying* at the feet of Gamaliel. Taught according to the perfect manner of the law of the fathers, and was zealous toward God, as ye all are this day.

4.   And I persecuted this *New* Way unto the death. Binding and *even* delivering into prisons both men and women.

5.   As also the high priest *this day* doth bear me witness, and all the estate of the elders. From whom also I received letters unto the brethren, and went *un*to Damascus, to bring them which were there *following this New Way* bound unto Jerusalem, for to be punished.

6.   And it came to pass, that, as I made my journey, and was come nigh unto Damascus about *the* noon *hour*, suddenly

there shone from *the* heaven a great light round about me.

7. And I fell unto the ground, and heard a voice saying unto me, "Saul, Saul, why persecutest thou me?"

8. And I answered *the voice*, Who art thou, Lord? And he said unto me, "I am Jesus of Nazareth, whom thou persecutest."

9. And they that were with me saw indeed the light, and were afraid. But they heard not the voice of him that spake *directly* to me.

10. And I said, What shall I do Lord? And the Lord said unto me, "Arise, and go into Damascus, and there it shall be told *to* thee of all *of* the things which are appointed for thee to do."

11. And when I could not see *with mine eyes* for the glory of that light, being *then* led by the hand of them that were with me, I came into Damascus.

12. And one *named* Ananias, *who was* a devout man according to the law *of Moses*, having a good report of all *of* the Jews which dwelt *there*,

13. Came unto me, and stood *before me*, and said unto me, Brother Saul, receive thy

sight. And the same hour I looked up upon him, *my sight being restored.*

14.   And he said *unto me*, The God of our fathers hath chosen thee, that thou shouldest know his will, and see that Just One, and shouldest *even* hear the voice of his mouth.

15.   For thou shalt be his witness unto all men of what thou hast seen and heard, *and what he will yet teach thee.*

16.   And now, why tarriest thou *any longer?* Arise, and be baptized *in water*, and wash away thy sins, calling *up*on the name of the Lord *Jesus.*

17.   And it came to pass, that, when I was come again to Jerusalem *over three years later*, even while I prayed in the temple, I was in a trance.

18.   And I saw him saying unto me, "Make haste, and get thee quickly out of Jerusalem, for *even* they *which believe in me* will not receive thy testimony concerning me."

19.   And I *protested and* said, Lord, they know that *in days gone by* I imprisoned and beat in every synagogue them that believed on thee.

20.   And *even* when the blood of thy martyr Stephen was shed, I also was standing by,

and consenting unto his death, and *further* kept the raiment of them that slew him.

21.   And he said unto me, "*Nevertheless,* depart. For I will send thee far hence unto the Gentiles."

22.   And they gave him audience unto this word, and *then* lifted up their voices, and said, Away with such a *fellow* from the earth, for it is not *even* fit that he should live!

23.   And as they cried out, and *began to* cast off *their* clothes, and threw dust *up* into the air,

24.   The chief captain commanded him to be brought into the castle, and bade that he should be *further* examined by scourging *him, so* that he might know wherefore *the* reason *that* they cried so against him.

25.   And as they bound him with thongs, *and were about to scourge him*, Paul said unto the centurion that *was put in charge and* stood by, Is it lawful for you to scourge a man that is a Roman *citizen*, and uncondemned *by any court?*

26.   When the centurion heard *those words*, he went and told the chief captain, saying, Take heed what thou *choose to* doest, for *I have learned that* this man is a Roman *citizen*.

27. Then the chief captain *hurried and* came, and said unto him, Tell me *the* truth, art thou a Roman citizen? *And* he said, Yea.

28. And the chief captain answered, With a great sum *of money* obtained I this freedom. And Paul *answered and* said *unto him*, But I was *free* born.

29. Then straightway they *who were about to scourge him* departed from him, *and those* which should have examined him *further*. And the chief captain *himself* also was afraid, after he knew that he was a Roman *citizen*, and because he had bound him.

30. On the morrow, because *it was expected that* he would have known the certainty wherefore he was accused of the Jews, he loosed him from *his* bands, and commanded the *Jewish* chief priests and all *of* their council to appear. And *when they had all arrived he* brought Paul down *from his cell*, and set him before them.

CHAPTER 23

1. And Paul, earnestly beholding the council, said *unto them*, Men *and* brethren, I have lived in all good conscience before *our* God until this day.

2. And *when Paul began to speak,* the high priest Ananias commanded them that stood by him to smite him on the mouth.

3. Then said Paul unto him, God shall smite thee *as well,* **thou** whited wall. For sittest thou to judge me after the law *of Moses,* and commandest me to be smitten contrary to the law?

4. And they that stood by *and heard this* said, Revilest thou God's *sanctioned* high priest?

5. Then said Paul, I wist not, brethren, that he was the high priest, *please forgive me.* For it is written, "Thou shalt not speak evil of the ruler of thy people." *(Exodus 22:28)*

6. But when Paul perceived that the one part *of the council* were Sadducees, and the other *part were* Pharisees, he cried out *with*in the council *with a loud voice,* Men **and** brethren, I am a Pharisee, *and* the son of a Pharisee. *It is* of the hope and resurrection of the dead *that* I am called in*to* question *this day.*

7. And when he had so said, there arose a dissension between the Pharisees and the Sadducees, and the multitude *of the people* was divided.

8.   For the Sadducees say that there is no resurrection *of the dead,* neither *are there* angel*s,* nor *that which is of the* spirit. But the Pharisees confess both.

9.   And there arose a great cry. And the scribes *that were* of the Pharisees' part arose, and strove *with the council,* saying, We find no evil in this man. But if a spirit or an angel hath spoken to him, let us not fight against God.

10.   And when there arose a great dissension, the chief captain, fearing lest Paul should have been pulled in*to* pieces of them, *finally* commanded the soldiers to go down *into the council,* and to take him by force from among them, and to bring *him* *once again* into the castle.

11.   And the night following *the tumult* the *New Creation* Lord *Jesus* stood by him, and said *unto him,* "Be of good cheer, *my brother* Paul, for as thou hast *faithfully* testified of me in Jerusalem, so must thou bear witness *of me* also at Rome."

12.   And when it was day, certain of the *unbelieving* Jews banded together, and bound themselves under a curse, saying *amongst themselves* that they would neither eat nor drink *un*til they had killed Paul.

13. And they were more than forty *in number* which had made this conspiracy.

14. And they came *boldly* to the chief priests and *the* elders *of the Sadducees*, and said *unto them*, We have bound ourselves *together* under a great curse, that we will eat nothing until we have slain Paul.

15. Now therefore ye with *the help of* the *whole* council signify to the *Roman* chief captain that he bring him down unto you tomorrow, as though ye would inquire something more perfectly concerning him. And we, *when he arrives* or ever he come near, are ready to kill him *on the spot*.

16. And when *a relative of* Paul's, *his* sister's son, *over*heard of their lying in wait, he went and entered in*to* the castle *to visit*, and *there* told Paul *of what they were planning*.

17. Then Paul called one of the centurions *over* unto *him*, and said *to him*, Bring this young man unto the chief captain, for he hath a certain thing to tell him.

18. So he took him, and brought *him* to the chief captain, and said, Paul the prisoner called me unto *him*, and prayed me to bring this young man unto thee, who hath something to say unto thee.

19. Then the chief captain took him by the hand, and went *with him* aside privately, and asked *of him*, What is *it* that thou hast to tell me?

20. And he said *unto him*, *I overheard that* the Jews have agreed to desire thee, that thou wouldest bring down Paul tomorrow into the council, as though they would inquire somewhat of him more perfectly.

21. But *I beg thee sir,* do not thou yield unto them. For there lie in wait for him of them more than forty men, which have bound themselves with an oath, that they will neither eat nor drink *aught* till they have killed him. And *even* now are they ready, looking for a promise from thee.

22. So the chief captain *then* let the young man depart, and charged *him saying,* See *that* *thou* tell no man that thou hast shown these things to me.

23. And *after the boy departed* he called unto *him* two centurions, saying, Make ready *immediately* two hundred soldiers to go to Caesarea, and *assemble* horsemen *of* threescore and ten, and *also* spearmen *of* two hundred, *and* at the third hour of the night *have them ready to go.*

24. And provide *for them* beasts, that they may set Paul on, and bring *him* safe unto Felix the governor *of Caesarea*.

25. And he wrote a letter *to Felix* after this manner:

26. Claudius Lysias unto the most excellent governor Felix: greeting*s to you*.

27. This man *that I am sending unto you* was taken of the Jews, and should have been killed of them. Then *when I heard of the uproar* came I with an army, and rescued him, having understood that he was a Roman *citizen*.

28. And when I would have known *further* the cause wherefore they *had* accused him, I brought him forth into their council.

29. *Of* whom I *then* perceived *that he was one* to be accused of *various* questions of their *own* law, but to have nothing *really* laid to his charge worthy of death or of bonds.

30. And when it was told *to* me how that the Jews *then* laid wait for the man, I sent *him* straightway to thee, and gave commandment to his accusers also to *appear and* say before thee what *they had* against him. Farewell.

31. Then the soldiers, as it was commanded them, took Paul, and brought *him* by night to *the city of* Antipatris.

32. On the morrow they left the *seventy* horsemen to *continue to* go with him, and *the remainder of the soldiers* returned *un*to the castle.

33. Who, when they came to Caesarea, and *personally* delivered the epistle to the governor, presented Paul also before him.

34. And when the governor had read *the letter*, he asked of *Paul of* what province *that* he was *from*. And when *Paul answered him* he understood that *he was* of *the province of* Cilicia.

35. I will hear *from* thee, said he, when thine accusers are also come *before me*. And he commanded him to be kept in Herod's judgment hall.

CHAPTER 24

1. And after five days, Ananias the high priest descended with the elders, and *also with* a certain orator *named* Tertullus, who *when they were brought before Felix*, informed the governor against Paul.

2. And when he was called forth, Tertullus began to accuse *him*, saying,

Seeing that by thee we enjoy great quietness, and that very worthy deeds are done unto this nation by thy providence,

3. We accept *it* always, and in all places, most noble Felix, with all thankfulness.

4. Notwithstanding, that I be not *any* further tedious unto thee, I pray thee that thou wouldest *bear with, and* hear us of thy clemency, *but* a few words.

5. For we have found this man *a* pestilent *fellow indeed*, and a mover of sedition among all *of* the Jews throughout the *whole* world, and *that he is* a ringleader of the sect of the Nazarenes.

6. Who also hath gone about to *purpose to* profane the temple *of our worship*. Whom we took, and would have judged *him* according to our law.

7. But the chief captain *Claudius* Lysias came *in upon us*, and with great violence took *him* away, *and* out of our hands.

8. Commanding his accusers to come *here to Caesarea* unto thee. By examining of whom *I speak* thyself, mayest take knowledge of all these things, whereof we *do* accuse him.

9. And *all of the other unconverted* **Jews** also assented, saying that these things were *indeed* so.

10. Then Paul, after that the governor had beckoned unto him *for* to speak, answered, Forasmuch as I know that thou hast been of many years a judge unto this nation *governor Felix*, I do the more cheerfully answer for myself.

11. *I would you to know,* because that thou mayest understand, that there are yet but *only* twelve days since I *originally* went up to Jerusalem for to worship.

12. And they neither found me in the temple disputing with any man, neither raising up the people, neither in the synagogues, nor in the city.

13. Neither can they prove the things whereof they now accuse me.

14. But this I *do* confess unto thee *Excellency*, that after the *New* **Way**, which they call heresy, so worship I the God of my fathers. Believing all *of the* things which are written in the law *of Moses*, and in the *writings of the* prophets.

15. And have *I* hope toward God, which they themselves also allow, that there shall be a resurrection of the dead, both of the just and *of the* unjust.

16.   And herein do I exercise myself, to *purpose to* have always a conscience void of offense toward God, and *toward* men.

17.   Now *again*, after many years, I came to bring alms to my nation, and offerings *unto my God.*

18.   Whereupon certain Jews from Asia found me purified in the temple, *in accordance with the law of Moses*, neither with *a* multitude, nor with *any* tumult.

19.   Who *themselves* ought to have been here before thee, and object, if they had aught against me.

20.   Or else let these same *men that are* **here** say, if they have found any evildoing in me, while I stood before the council,

21.   Except it be for this one voice, that I cried *out* standing among them, touching *the hope of* the resurrection of the dead. *It is for that reason that* I am called in question by you this day.

22.   And when Felix heard these things, having *a* more perfect knowledge of *that New* Way, he deferred them, and said *unto them,* When *Claudius* Lysias the chief captain

shall come down *from Jerusalem*, I will know the uttermost of your matter.

23.   And he commanded a centurion to keep Paul, and to let *him* have *his* liberty, and that he should forbid none of his acquaintance to minister or come unto *visit* him.

24.   And after certain days, when Felix came *in to the judgment hall* with his wife Drusilla, which was *herself* a Jewess, he sent for Paul, and heard him concerning the faith *that he exercised* in Christ.

25.   And as he reasoned of *the* righteousness *of Christ*, and *of* temperance, and *of the* judgment to come, Felix trembled, and answered, Go thy way for this time, *and* when I have a *more* convenient season, I will call for thee *again*.

26.   He hoped also that *bribery* money should have been given *unto* him of Paul, that he might loose him. Wherefore he sent for him the oftener, and communed with him.

27.   But after *the passing of* two years *time*, Porcius Festus came *unto Caesarea, and came* into Felix's room. And Felix, willing to show the *unconverted* Jews a pleasure, *and trying to impress Festus*, left Paul bound.

CHAPTER 25

1.   Now when Festus was come into the province *again*, after three days he ascended from Caesarea to Jerusalem.

2.   Then the high priest and the chief *rulers* of the Jews informed him against Paul, and besought him,

3.   And desired *that he would give them* favour against him, *and* that he would send *to Caesarea* for him to *come unto* Jerusalem, laying wait in the way *for* to kill him.

4.   But Festus answered, that Paul should be kept at Caesarea, and that he himself would depart shortly *to go* **thither.**

5.   Let them therefore, said he, which among you are able, go down with *me*, and accuse this man *in person*, if there be any wickedness *per chance* in him.

6.   And when he had tarried among them more than ten days, he went down unto Caesarea *again*. And the next day *while* sitting on the judgment seat *he* commanded Paul to be brought.

7.   And when he was come *before him*, the *unconverted* Jews which came down from Jerusalem stood round about and laid

many *accusations* and grievous complaints against Paul, which they could not prove.

8. While he answered for himself, Neither against the *Mosaic* law of the Jews, *yea* neither against the *sacredness of the* temple, nor yet against Caesar *himself,* have I offended any thing at all.

9. But Festus, willing to do the *unbelieving* Jews a pleasure, answered Paul, and said, Wilt thou go up to Jerusalem, and there be judged of these things *presented against thee,* before me?

10. Then said Paul, I stand at Caesar's judgment seat, where I ought to be judged *as a Roman citizen.* To the Jews have I done no wrong, as thou very well knowest.

11. For if I be an offender *of any law,* or have committed any thing worthy of *being put to* death, I refuse not to die. But if there be *substance to* none of these things whereof these accuse me, no man may deliver me unto them. I appeal unto Caesar.

12. Then Festus, when he had conferred with the council, answered, Hast thou appealed unto Caesar? *Then* unto Caesar shalt thou go.

13.   And after *a* certain *number of* days king
Agrippa and Bernice, *the wife of Agrippa's uncle,*
came unto Caesarea to salute Festus.

14.   And when they had been there many
days, Festus declared Paul's cause unto the
king, saying, There is a certain man *who has
been* left in bonds *for a long time* by Felix.

15.   About whom, when I was at
Jerusalem, the *Jewish* chief priests and the
elders informed *me*, desiring *to have* me give
them judgment against him.

16.   To whom I answered, It is not the
manner of the Roman's *law* to deliver any
man to die, before that he which is accused
have *met* the accusers face to face, and have
been given license to answer for himself
concerning the crime laid against him.

17.   Therefore, when they were come
hither *to Caesarea*, without any delay, on the
morrow I sat on the judgment seat, and
commanded the man to be brought forth.

18.   Against whom, when the accusers
stood up *for to testify*, they brought *forth* none
accusation of such things as I supposed.

19.   But had *only* certain questions *to pose*
against him of their own *religious*
superstition, and of one *named* Jesus, which
was dead, whom Paul affirmed to be alive.

20. And because I doubted of such manner of questions, I asked *him* whether he would go to Jerusalem, and there be judged of these matters.

21. But when Paul *declined to go back to Jerusalem and* had appealed to be reserved unto the hearing of Augustus, I commanded him to be kept *in custody* till I might send him to Caesar.

22. Then Agrippa said unto Festus, I would also *like to* hear the man myself. Tomorrow, said he, thou shalt hear him.

23. And on the morrow when Agrippa was come, and Bernice, with great pomp, and was entered into the place of hearing, with the chief captains, and *the* principal men of the city, at Festus' commandment Paul was brought forth.

24. And Festus said, *excellent* King Agrippa, and all men which are here present with us, ye see this man, about whom all *of* the multitude of the Jews have dealt with me, both at Jerusalem, and *also* here, crying *out unto me* that he ought not to live any longer.

25. But when I found *out* that he had committed nothing worthy of death *according to Roman law*, and that *being a Roman citizen* he himself hath appealed *un*to Augustus, I have determined to send him *to Rome.*

26.   Of whom I have no certain thing to write unto my lord *Caesar.* Wherefore I have brought him forth before you, and specially before thee, O king Agrippa, that, after examination *being* had, I might have somewhat to write.

27.   For it seemeth to me *an* unreasonable *thing* to send a prisoner, and not withal to signify *of* the crimes *that are* **laid** against him.

CHAPTER 26

1.   Then Agrippa said unto Paul, Thou art permitted to speak for thyself. Then Paul stretched forth the hand, and answered for himself.

2.   I think myself *quite* happy, king Agrippa, because I shall answer for myself this day before thee, touching all *of* the things whereof I am accused of the Jews.

3.   Especially *because I know* thee to be *an* expert in all *of the* customs and questions which are among the Jews. Wherefore I beseech thee to hear me patiently.

4. My manner of life from my youth, which was at the first, among mine own nation at Jerusalem, know all *of* the Jews *that are gathered here.*

5. Which knew me from the beginning, if they would *be willing to* testify, that after the most straitest sect of our religion I lived, *as* a Pharisee.

6. And now I stand and am judged *by these same people* for the hope of the promise *that was* made of God unto our fathers.

7. Unto which *promise* our twelve tribes, instantly serving *the living* **God** day and night, hope to come. For which hope's sake, king Agrippa, I am accused of the Jews *here gathered.*

8. Why should it be thought a thing incredible with you, that *the living* **God** should raise the dead?

9. I verily thought with myself *at one time,* that I ought to do many *unsavory* things contrary to the name of Jesus of Nazareth.

10. Which thing I also did *starting* in Jerusalem. And many of the saints *of the* *Lord Jesus* did I shut up in*to* prison, having received authority from the chief priests *to do so.* And when they were put to death,

supposedly under the law of Moses, **I gave** my voice **against** *them,* *as these do here, against me, today.*

11. And I punished them oft*en* in every synagogue, and compelled *them* to blaspheme. And being exceedingly mad against them, I persecuted *them* even unto strange cities.

12. Whereupon as I went to Damascus with *legal* authority and commission from the chief priests,

13. At midday, O king, I saw in the way a light from heaven, above the brightness of the sun, shining round about me, and them which journeyed with me.

14. And when we were all fallen *from our horses* to the earth, I heard a voice speaking unto me, and saying in the Hebrew tongue, "Saul, Saul, why persecutest thou me? it is hard for thee to kick against the pricks."

15. And I said, Who art thou, Lord? And he said, "I am Jesus whom thou persecutest.

16. But rise, and stand upon thy feet. For I have appeared unto thee for this purpose, to make thee a minister and a witness, both of these things which thou hast seen, and of

those things in the which I will appear unto thee.

17.　Delivering thee from the people, and *from* the Gentiles, unto whom now I send thee.

18.　To open their eyes, *and* to turn *them* from darkness to light. And *from* the power of Satan unto God, that they may receive forgiveness of sins, and inheritance among them which are sanctified by faith that is in me."

19.　Whereupon, O king Agrippa, I was not disobedient unto the heavenly vision.

20.　But showed *what the Lord shared with me* first unto them of Damascus, and *then* at Jerusalem, and throughout all the coasts of Judea, and *then* to the Gentiles, that they should repent and turn to *the living* God, and do works meet for repentance.

21.　For these causes the *unbelieving* Jews caught me in the temple *fulfilling a vow*, and went about to kill *me*.

22.　Having therefore obtained help of God, I continue unto this *very* day, witnessing both to small and great, saying none other things than those which the prophets and Moses did say should come.

23.   That *the* Christ should suffer, *and* that he should be the first *individual* that should rise from the *spiritual* dead, and *that he* should show light unto the people *of God*, and to the Gentiles.

24.   And as he thus spake for himself, Festus *was stirred from within himself and* said with a loud voice, Paul, thou art beside thyself, much learning doth make thee mad.

25.   But he said, I am not mad *at all*, most noble Festus, but speak forth the words of truth and soberness.

26.   For the king *truly* knowth of these things, before whom also I speak freely. For I am persuaded that none of these things are hidden from him. For this thing was not done in *some darkened room, or in* a corner.

27.   *Then Paul said,* King Agrippa, believest thou the prophets?

28.   Then Agrippa said unto Paul, Almost thou persuades me to be a Christian.

29.   And Paul said, I would to God, that not only thou *king Agrippa*, but also all that *can* hear me this day, were both almost, and altogether such as I am, except *for* these bonds.

30. And when he had thus spoken *his heart*, the king rose up, and the governor, and Bernice, and *all* they that sat with them.

31. And when they were gone aside, they talked between themselves, saying, This man doeth nothing worthy of death or of bonds.

32. Then said Agrippa unto Festus, This man might have been set at liberty, if he had not appealed unto Caesar.

CHAPTER 27

1. And when it was determined that *Paul should be sent to Rome, and that* we should *set* sail *to go* into Italy, they delivered Paul and certain other prisoners unto *one* named Julius, *who was* a *Roman* centurion of Augustus' band.

2. And entering into a ship *bound for the city* of Adramyttium, we launched, meaning to sail by the coasts of Asia, *with* **one** Aristarchus, a Macedonian of Thessalonica, being *on board* with us.

3. And the next *day* we touched *land* at *the seaport city of* Sidon. And Julius courteously entreated Paul, and *chose to* give *him* liberty to go unto his friends, *in order* to refresh himself.

4.   And when we had launched from thence, we sailed under *the island of* Cyprus, because the winds were contrary.

5.   And when we had sailed over the sea of Cilicia and Phamphylia, we came to Myra, *a city* of Lycia.

6.   And there the centurion found a ship *that was* of Alexandria, *which was* sailing into Italy, and he put *all of* us therein.

7.   And when we had sailed slowly *for* many days, and scarce were *able to* come over against *the city of* Cnidus, the wind was not suffering us, we sailed unto *the island of* Crete, over against *the area of* Salmone.

8.   And, hardly passing it *with difficulty*, came unto a place which is called the Fair Havens, nigh whereunto was the city *of* Lasea.

9.   Now, when much time was spent *with these maneuvers*, and when sailing was now *becoming more* dangerous, because the Feast *of the Day of Atonement*, was now already past, Paul admonished *the company*.

10.   And he said unto them, Sirs, I perceive *by the Spirit of grace* that this voyage will be *fraught* with hurt and much damage,

not only of the lading and *the* ship, but also of our *own* lives.

11.   Nevertheless the centurion believed the master *of the vessel* and the owner of the ship, more *so* then those things which were spoken *of* by Paul.

12.   And because the haven *itself* was not commodious to winter in, the more part *of the harbor directors* advised *us* to depart thence also. *Counseling* if by any means, *that* they might attain to *the seaport city of* Phenice, **and there** *to be able* to winter. **Which** *actually* **is** a *port of* haven of *the island of* Crete, and lieth toward the southwest and *the* northwest.

13.   And when the south wind blew softly, *the masters* supposing that they had obtained **their** purpose, *and* loosing **thence** *from the Fair Havens*, they sailed close by *the isle of* Crete.

14.   But not long after *the ship departed* there arose against it a tempestuous wind, called Euroclydon.

15.   And when the ship was caught *in the hurricane*, and could not bear up *and make any forward progress sailing* into the wind, we *turned her around and* let **her** drive.

16.   And running under a certain island which is called Clauda, we had much work

to do, to land the skiff, and **to** *finally* **come by the boat.**

17. **Which when they had taken** *her* **up** *into the ship,* **they used** *the cable* **helps** *in* **undergirding the ship. And fearing lest they should fall into the quicksands** *and run aground,* *they* **struck sail, and so were driven** *by the wind.*

18. **And we being exceedingly tossed with a tempest, the next** *day* **they lightened the ship.**

19. **And the third** *day* **we cast out, with our own hands, the tackling of the ship.**

20. **And when neither** *the* **sun nor** *the* **stars in many days appeared, and** *it became clear that* **no small tempest lay** *up*on **us,** **all hope that we should be saved was then taken away.**

21. **But after** *a* **long abstinence, Paul stood forth in the midst of them, and said** *boldly,* **Sirs, ye should have hearkened unto me** *when I spoke,* **and not have loosed from Crete. And** *having not listened then,* **to have** *thus* **gained this harm and loss** *as a result.*

22. **And now I exhort you** *once again,* **to be of good cheer. For there shall be no loss of any man's life among you, but** *I cannot say the same* **of the ship.**

23.   For there stood by me this *very* night the angel of *the living* God, whose I am, and whom I serve.

24.   Saying *unto me*, Fear not, Paul, *for* thou must be brought before Caesar. And, lo, God hath given thee all them that sail with thee, *prisoner and crewman alike.*

25.   Wherefore, sirs, be of good cheer. For I believe God, that it shall be *done* even as it was told *unto* me.

26.   Howbeit, *in the process,* we must be cast upon a certain island.

27.   But when the fourteenth night was come, as we were *being* driven up and down in *the* Adria*tic Sea,* about *the* midnight *hour* the shipmen deemed that they drew near to some country.

28.   And *they* sounded, and found *it to be* twenty fathoms. And when they had gone a little further, they sounded again, and found *it to be* fifteen fathoms.

29.   Then fearing lest we should have fallen upon *some* rocks, they cast four anchors out of the stern *of the ship*, and wished for the day*light to come.*

30.   And as the shipmen were about to flee out of the ship, when they had let down the *life*boat into the sea, under colour

as though they would have cast *some more* anchors out of the foreship,

31.   Paul said to the centurion and to the soldiers *with him*, Except these *crewmen* abide *with*in the ship, ye cannot be saved.

32.   Then the soldiers *intervened and* cut off the ropes of the *life*boat, and let her fall off.

33.   And while the day was coming on, Paul besought *them* all to take *of some* meat. Saying, This day is the fourteenth day that ye have tarried and continued fasting, having taken nothing.

34.   Wherefore I pray you to take *some* meat. For this is for your health. For there shall not a hair fall from the head of any of you.

35.   And when he had thus spoken, he took *some* bread, and gave thanks *un*to God in *the* presence of them all, and when he had broken *it*, he began to eat.

36.   Then were they all of good cheer, and they also took *some* meat.

37.   And we were in all *with*in the ship two hundred threescore and sixteen souls *in number.*

38.   And when they *all* had eaten enough *to strengthen themselves*, they lightened the ship, and cast out the wheat *cargo* into the sea.

39. And when it was day, they knew not the land, but they discovered a certain creek with a shore, into the which they were minded, if it were possible to thrust in the ship.

40. And when they had taken up the anchors *from the stern of the ship*, they committed *themselves* unto the *tides of the* sea. And *they* loosed the rudder bands, and hoisted up the mainsail *in*to the wind, and made toward *the* shore *that they had seen.*

41. And falling into a place where two seas met, they ran the ship aground. And the forepart stuck fast *in the sand*, and remained unmovable, but the hinder part was broken *up* with the violence of the waves *beating against it.*

42. And the *other* soldiers' counsel *to the centurion* was to kill the prisoners, lest any of them should swim out *to the sea*, and escape.

43. But the centurion, willing to save *the prisoner* Paul, kept them from *their* purpose. And *he* commanded that they which could swim should cast *themselves* first *into the sea*, and get to land.

44. And the rest *of the prisoners and the crew were to make their way*, some on boards, and some on *broken pieces* of the ship. And so

it came to pass, *even as the angel had promised to Paul,* that they escaped all safe to the land.

CHAPTER 28

1.   And when they were *all* escaped *from the shipwreck,* then they knew that the *name of the* island as *the natives* called *it, was* Melita.

2.   And the barbarous people *of the island* showed us no little kindness. For they kindled *for us* a fire, and received us every one *into a shelter,* because of the present rain, and because of the cold.

3.   And when Paul had gathered a bundle of sticks, and laid *them* on the fire, there came a viper *snake* out of the heat *of the fire,* and fastened *itself* on*to* his hand.

4.   And when the barbarians *of the island* saw the *venomous* beast hang on*to* his hand, they said among themselves, No doubt this man is a murderer, whom, though he hath escaped *from* the sea, yet vengeance suffereth *him* not to live.

5.   And he shook off the beast *from his hand* into the fire, and felt no harm.

6.   Howbeit they *continually* looked *to see* when he should have swollen *up,* or fallen

down dead suddenly. But after they had looked *for* a great while, and saw no harm come to him, they changed their minds, and said *instead* that he was a god *of some sort.*

7.   In the same quarters *where we stayed,* were *the personal* possessions of the chief man of the island, whose name was Publius. *The same is he* who received us, and lodged us three days courteously.

8.   And it came to pass, that the father of Publius lay sick *at his house* of a fever and of a bloody flux. To whom Paul entered in, and prayed *for*, and laid his hands on him, and healed him.

9.   So when this was done, others also, which had diseases, *and had heard of Paul* in the island, came, and were healed.

10.   Who also honoured us with many honours. And when we departed *from the village*, they laded *us* with such things as were necessary *for our journey.*

11.   And after three months *time* we departed in a ship of Alexandria, which had *also* wintered in the isle, whose *zodiac* sign was Castor and Pollux, *which are the Gemini twins.*

12.   And landing at *the city of* Syracuse, we tarried *there for* three days.

13. And from thence we fetched a compass, and came to *the city of* **Rhegium**. And after one day the south wind blew, and we came the next day to *the city of* **Puteoli**, *which was on the Bay of Naples, in Italy.*

14. Where we found brethren *of the Lord,* and were desired *by them* to tarry with them *for* seven days. And so *after our visitation,* we went toward **Rome**.

15. And from thence, when the *other* brethren heard of us, they came to meet us *from* as far *away* as *the town of* **Appi Forum**, and *from* the *town of* **Three Taverns**. Whom when Paul saw, he *rejoiced and* thanked **God**, and took courage.

16. And when we *finally* came to Rome, the centurion delivered the prisoners to the captain of the guard. But Paul was suffered to dwell by himself, with a soldier that kept *guard over* him.

17. And it came to pass, that after three days Paul called the chief *leaders* of the Jews *that were in Rome* together. And when they were come together, he said unto them, Men *and* brethren, though I have committed nothing against the people, or customs of our fathers, yet was I delivered

as a prisoner from Jerusalem, into the hands of the Romans.

18.   Who, when they had examined me, would have let *me* go, because *that* there was no cause of death *with*in me.

19.   But when the Jews *of Jerusalem* spake against *it*, I was constrained to appeal unto Caesar *because of my Roman citizenry.* Not that I had aught to accuse my nation of.

20.   For this cause therefore have I called for you, to see *you*, and to speak with *you*. Because that *it is* for the hope of Israel, *as is prophesied in the Scriptures, that* I am bound with this chain.

21.   And they said unto him, We neither received *any* letters out of Judea concerning thee, neither *have* any of the brethren that came *from outside of Rome* showed or spake *of* any harm *that is come* of thee.

22.   But we desire to hear of thee what thou *really* thinkest. For as concerning this *new* sect, we know that every where it is spoken against *by the people of our nation.*

23.   And when they had appointed him a *certain* day, there came many *un*to him into *his* lodging. To whom he expounded and testified *concerning* the kingdom of God. Persuading them concerning *New Creation*

Jesus, both out of the law of Moses, and *out of* the prophets, from *the* morning till *the* evening.

24.   And some believed the things which were spoken *of by Paul,* and some believed not.

25.   And when they agreed not among themselves, they departed *from his lodging,* after that Paul had spoken one *final* word. Well spake the Holy Ghost by Isaiah the prophet unto our fathers,

26.   Saying, "Go unto this people, and say, Hearing ye shall hear, and shall not understand. And seeing ye shall see, and not perceive.

27.   For the heart of this people is waxed gross, and their ears are dull of hearing, and their eyes have they closed. Lest they should see with *their* eyes, and hear with *their* ears, and understand with *their* heart, and should be converted, and I should heal them." *(Isaiah 6:9-10)*

28.   Be it known therefore unto you, that the salvation of God is sent unto the Gentiles, and that they will hear it.

29.   And when he had said these words *to them,* the Jews departed, and had great reasoning among themselves.

30. And Paul dwelt *another* two whole years in his own hired house *awaiting his being brought before Caesar.* **And** *he openly* received all that came in unto him.

31. Preaching the kingdom of God, and teaching *all* those things which concern the *New Creation* **Lord Jesus Christ,** with all confidence. *And there was* no man forbidding him, *neither Jew nor Gentile.*

THE BOOK OF
JAMES

CHAPTER 1

1. James, a *willing* servant of God, and *half-brother* of the *New Creation* Lord Jesus Christ, to *the New Creation converts from* the twelve tribes *of Israel* which are scattered abroad, greeting.

2. My brethren, count it all joy when ye fall into divers temptations.

3. Knowing *this*, that the trying of your faith, *which is much more precious that gold,* worketh patience.

4. But let patience have *her* perfect work *in you,* that *when it is finished,* ye may be perfect and entire, wanting nothing.

5. If any of you *seemeth to* lack wisdom *that comes from above,* let him ask of God, that giveth to all *men* liberally, and unbraideth not, and it shall be given *unto* him.

6. But let him ask in faith, nothing wavering. For he that wavereth *back and forth in his dealings* is like a wave of the sea driven with the wind and tossed.

7.   For let not that man *even* think that he shall receive any thing of the Lord.

8.   *The fact of the matter is, that* a double-minded man *is* unstable in all *of* his ways.

9.   Let the brother of low degree rejoice in that he is exalted *in Christ Jesus.*

10.   But the rich *man should rejoice* in *his humility*, that he is made low. Because as the flower of the grass *is here one day and gone the next*, he *too* shall pass away.

11.   For the *morning* sun is no sooner risen with a burning heat, but it withereth the grass. And the *blossoming* flower thereof falleth, and the grace of the fashion of it*s beauty* perisheth. So also shall the rich man *on this earth* fade away in his *own* ways.

12.   Blessed *is* the man that *submitteth himself unto God, and* endureth temptation. For when he is tried *at the Bema Seat of Christ Jesus*, he shall receive the crown of life, which the Lord hath promised to them that love him.

13.   Let no man say when he is tempted *in any manner, that* I am tempted of God. For God cannot be tempted with *any type of* evil, neither tempteth he any man.

14.　But every man is tempted, when he is drawn away of his own *personal* lust, and enticed.

15.　Then when *that* lust hath conceived *and is acted upon*, it bringeth forth sin. And sin, when it is finished *running its course*, bringeth forth death.

16.　Do not err, my beloved brethren *in understanding that,*

17.　*Only* every good gift and every perfect gift is from above. And *they* cometh down from the Father of lights *in heaven*, with whom is no variableness, neither *even a* shadow of turning.

18.　Of his own *free* will begat he us with the *faith of the living* word of truth, that we should be a kind of firstfruits of his *New Creation* creatures.

19.　Wherefore, my beloved brethren, let every man *purpose to* be swift to hear, *but* slow to speak, *and* slow to wrath.

20.　For the wrath of *the natural* man worketh not the righteousness of God.

21.　Wherefore lay apart all *carnal* filthiness and superfluity of naughtiness, and *be willing to* receive with meekness the engrafted word *of God*, which is able to save your souls *from damnation*.

22.　But *put action to your faith and* be ye doers of the word, and not hearers only, deceiving your own selves.

23.　For if any *man* be *only* a hearer of the word, and not a doer, he is like unto a man beholding his natural face in a *mirrored* glass.

24.　For he beholdeth himself, and goeth *along* his way, and straightway forgeteth what manner of man he was.

25.　But whoso looketh into the perfect law of liberty, *which is the Word of God,* and continueth *therein,* he being not a forgetful hearer, but a doer of the work, this man shall be blessed *by God* in his deed.

26.　If any man among you seem*eth* to be *a* religious *man,* and *yet* bridleth not his tongue, but *continues to* deceiveth his own heart, this man's religion *is* vain.

27.　*Genuinely* pure religion and undefiled *behaviour* before God and the Father is this, To visit the fatherless and *the* widows in their affliction, *and* to *purpose to* keep himself unspotted from the world.

CHAPTER 2

1.　My brethren, have not the *righteous* faith of our *New Creation* Lord Jesus Christ, *the Lord* of glory, *along* with *a* respect of persons.

2. For if there come unto your *church* assembly a man with a gold ring, *dressed* in goodly apparel, and there come in also a poor man *dressed* in vile raiment;

3. And ye have respect to him that weareth the gay clothing, and say unto him, Sit thou here in a good place. And *then you* say to the poor *man*, Stand thou there, or sit here under my footstool,

4. Are ye not then *become* partial *with*in yourselves, and are becom*ing* judges of evil thoughts?

5. Hearken, my beloved brethren, Hath not God *himself* chosen the poor of this world *who are* rich in faith and *love, to become the* heirs of the kingdom *of God* which he hath promised to them that love him?

6. But ye have despised the poor. Do not *the* rich men *of this world* oppress you, and *then* draw you before the judgment seats?

7. Do not they *speak against you and* blaspheme that worthy name by the which ye are called?

8. If ye *will* fulfill the Royal Law according to the Scripture, "Thou shalt love thy neighbor as thyself," *(Leviticus 19:18)* ye do well.

9. But if ye *choose to* have respect to persons, ye commit sin, and are convinced *even* of the law *of Moses* as transgressors.

10. For whosoever shall *try to* keep the whole law *of Moses*, and yet offend in one *small* **point**, he is guilty of *breaking it* all.

11. For he that said, "Do not commit adultery," said also "Do not kill." Now if thou commit no adultery, yet if thou kill, thou art become a transgressor of he law. *(Exodus 20:13-14)*

12. So speak ye, and so do, as they that shall be judged *not by the law of Moses, but* by the *perfect* law of liberty.

13. For he shall have judgment without mercy, *upon them* that hath shown no mercy. And *we know that* mercy rejoiceth against judgment.

14. What *doth it* profit *you* my brethren, though a man say *that* he hath faith, and have not *the* works *to go with it?* can faith *by itself* save him?

15. *What good is it* if a brother or *a* sister be naked *of clothing*, and destitute of daily food,

16. And one of you say unto them, Depart in peace, be *ye* warmed and filled. Notwithstanding ye give them not those

things which are needful to *clothe or to feed* the body, what *doth* it profit?

17.   Even so *your* faith, if it hath not works *to go with it*, is dead, being alone.

18.   Yea, a man may say *unto you*, Thou hast faith, and I have works. Show me thy faith without thy works, and I will show thee my faith by my works.

19.   Thou believest *and declare* that there is one God? Thou doest well. The devils *from the kingdom of darkness* also believe, and tremble.

20.   But wilt thou know *this*, O vain man, that faith without works *to go with it* is dead?

21.   Was not Abraham our father justified *before God* by works, when he had offered *up* Isaac his *only begotten* son *of promise* upon the altar?

22.   Seest thou how *his* faith *was* wrought with his works? And by *those* works was *his* faith made perfect.

23.   And the Scripture was fulfilled which saith, "Abraham believed God, and it was imputed unto him for righteousness," and he was called the Friend of God. *(Genesis 15:6)*

24.   Ye see then how that by works a man is justified *before God*, and not by faith only.

25. Likewise also was not Rahab the harlot justified by works, when she had received *and believed* the messengers, and had sent *them* out another way?

26. For as the *physical* body without the *indwelling* spirit *being there* is dead, so faith without works is dead also.

CHAPTER 3

1. My brethren, be *ye* not many masters, knowing that we shall receive the greater condemnation.

2. For in *attempting to be masters of* many things we offend all. If any man *will* offend not in *his* word, the same *is* a perfect man, *and* able also to bridle the whole body.

3. Behold, we put bits in the horses' mouths, that they may obey us; and we *may* turn about their whole body *using that bridle and bit.*

4. Behold, also the ships *of the sea,* which though *they be* so great, and *are* driven of fierce winds, yet are they turned about *and guided* with a very small helm, whithersoever the governor listeth.

5. Even so the tongue is a little member *within our body*, and boasteth great

things. Behold, how great a matter a little fire *at the first, is able to* kindleth!

6. And the tongue *that we have* is *indeed* a fire, a world *full* of iniquity. So is the tongue among *all of* our members, that it defileth the whole body, and *even* setteth on fire the course of nature. And *yet* it is set on fire of hell *itself.*

7. For every kind of beasts, and of birds, and of serpents, and of things in the sea, is tamed, and hath been tamed of mankind.

8. But the tongue *of a man* can no man tame *by himself.* **It is** an unruly evil, full of deadly poison.

9. Therewith, *with our own tongue,* bless we God, even the Father *in heaven.* And therewith, *with our own tongue,* curse we men *on this earth,* which are made after the similitude of *our* God *in heaven.*

10. Out of the same mouth proceedeth *this* blessing and *this* cursing. My brethren, these things ought not so to be.

11. Doth a fountain send forth at the *very* same place sweet *water* and bitter?

12. Can the fig tree, my brethren, bear olive berries? Either *can* a vine *bear* figs? So *can* no fountain both yield salt water and fresh *water at the same place.*

13. Who *proclaims that he* ***is*** a wise man and endued with knowledge among you? Let him *clearly* show out of a good conversation his *manifest* works, with meekness of wisdom.
14. But if ye have bitter envying and strife *with*in your hearts, glory not, and lie not against the truth.
15. This *kind of natural* wisdom descendeth not from above, but *is* earthly, *and* sensual, *and* devilish.
16. For *it is a demonstrated reality that* where envying and strife *is allowed*, there *is* confusion and every evil work.
17. But the wisdom that is from above*, and is resident within each person who is a recipient of the finished work of the cross,* is first pure, *and* then peaceable. *It is* gentle, ***and*** easy to be entreated, full of mercy and good fruits, without partiality, and without hypocrisy.
18. And the *manifested* fruit of righteousness is sown in peace, *as well as sown* of them that make peace.

CHAPTER 4

1. From whence *come* wars and fightings among you? *Come they* not hence, even of your *own personal* lust that war *with*in your *own* members?

2. Ye lust, and *have* not. Ye kill, and desire to have, and cannot obtain. Ye fight and war, yet ye have not, because ye ask not *the right person.*

3. Ye ask, and receive not, because ye *unrighteously* ask amiss, that ye may *be able to* consume *it* upon your *own* lusts.

4. Ye adulterers and adulteresses, know ye not that the friendship of the world, *which ye have established,* is *at* enmity with God? Whosoever therefore will *choose to* be a friend of the world is the enemy of God.

5. Do ye think that the Scripture saith in vain, "The spirit *of man* that dwelleth in us lusteth to envy?" *(Proverbs 21:10)*

6. But *because of his mercy* he giveth *us* more grace. Wherefore he saith, "God resisteth the proud, but giveth grace unto the humble." *(Proverbs 3:34)*

7. *Choose to* submit yourselves therefore *un*to God *and to the instruction that he gives us within his word. And* resist the devil *by following those instructions and becoming a doer of the word,* and he will flee from you.

8. Draw nigh to God, and *as* he *has promised, he* will draw nigh *un*to you. *I exhort*

you to cleanse *your* hands, *ye* sinners, and purify *your* hearts, *ye* double-minded.

9. Be afflicted, and mourn, and weep. Let your *current* laughter be turned *in*to mourning, and *your* joy *in*to heaviness *because of genuine repentance.*

10. Humble yourselves in the sight of the Lord, and *in due time* he shall lift you up.

11. Speak not evil one of another, brethren. He that speaketh evil of *his* brother, and judgeth his brother, speaketh evil of the law *that God hath given*, and judgeth the law *itself.* But if thou *set thyself up as a* judge *of* the law, thou art not a doer of the law *as you should be*, but a judge.

12. There is *only* one lawgiver, who is able to save and to destroy. Who art thou that judgest another?

13. Go to now, ye that *boast and* say, Today or tomorrow we will go into such a city, and continue there a year, and buy and sell, and get gain.

14. Whereas ye know not what *shall be* on the morrow. For what is *the sum of* your life? It is even *as* a vapour, that appeareth for a *very* little time, and then vanisheth away.

15. For that ye *ought* to say, If the Lord will, we shall live, and do this, or that.

16. But now ye rejoice in your boasting. All such rejoicing *and boasting* is evil.

17. Therefore to him that knoweth to do good, and doeth *it* not, to him it is sin.

CHAPTER 5

1. Go to now, *ye* rich men, weep and howl for your miseries that shall come upon *you.*

2. Your *earthly* riches are corrupted, and your *precious* garments are motheaten.

3. Your gold and *your* silver, *which ye have put your trust in* is cankered. And the rust of them shall be a witness against you, and shall eat your flesh as *if* it were fire. Ye have heaped *earthly* treasure together for the last days.

4. Behold, the *voices of the men you* hire *which are a part* of the labourers who have reaped down your fields, which is of you kept back by fraud, crieth. And the cries of them which have reaped *for you* are entered into the ears of the Lord of Sabaoth.

5. Ye have lived in pleasure *while you are* on the earth, and been wanton. Ye have nourished your hearts *with unrighteousness*, as in a day of slaughter.

6. Ye have condemned *and* killed the just *man, and* he doth not resist you.

7. Be patient therefore, *my* brethren, unto the coming of the Lord. Behold, the husbandman waiteth *a long time* for the precious fruit of the earth, and hath long patience for it, until he receive *both* the early and *the* latter rain.

8. Be ye also patient, *e*stablish your hearts *in righteousness*, for the coming of the Lord draweth nigh.

9. Grudge not one against another, brethren, lest ye be condemned. Behold, the *true* judge standeth before the door.

10. Take, my brethren, the prophets *who have lived in days gone by*, who have spoken in the name of the Lord, for an example of suffering affliction and of patience.

11. Behold, we *have* count*ed* them happy which *have* endure*d such afflictions*. Ye have heard of the patience of Job? And have seen *in the Scriptures* the end of the Lord*'s dealing with him*, that the Lord is very pitiful, and of tender mercy.

12. But above all *these* things, my brethren, *purpose to* swear not, neither by

heaven, neither by the earth, neither by any other oath. But let your *words of* yea be yea; and your *words of* nay, *be* nay, lest ye fall into condemnation.

13. Is *there* any among you *who is* afflicted? Let him *effectually* pray. Is *there* any merry? Let him sing *from the* psalms *a song unto the Lord.*

14. Is *there* any *physically* sick among you? Let him *first* call for the elders of the church. And let them *come and* pray over him, anointing him with oil in the name of the Lord.

15. And the prayer of faith shall *indeed* save the sick, and the Lord shall raise him up *from his bed of affliction.* And if he hath committed *any* sins, they shall be forgiven him.

16. Confess *your* faults *and shortcomings* one to another, and *then* pray one for another, that ye may be healed. *For* the effectual fervent prayer of a righteous man availeth much.

17. Elijah was a man subject to *the same* like passions as we are, and *yet* he prayed earnestly that it might not rain *in the land of Israel,* and it rained not on the earth *within that covenant land* by the space of three years

and six months.

18.   And he prayed again, and the heaven *responded and* gave *forth the* rain, and the earth brought forth her fruit.

19.   Brethren, if any of you do err from the truth, and one *counsel and* convert him *unto repentance,*

20.   Let him know, that he which converteth the sinner from the error of his way shall save a soul from *certain* death, and shall hide a multitude of sins.

THE BOOK OF
I PETER

CHAPTER 1

1.   Peter, an *ordained* apostle of *the New Creation* Jesus Christ *un*to the strangers scattered throughout *the regions of* Pontus, Galatia, Cappadocia, Asia, and Bithynia.

2.   *To every person* elect according to the *divine* foreknowledge of God the Father, *truly elected of God* through *the* sanctification *work* of the *Holy* Spirit, unto *your willing* obedience *to the gospel* and *the* sprinkling of the blood of Jesus Christ. Grace *be ministered* unto you, and *the* peace *of God,* be multiplied.

3.   Blessed *be* the God and Father of our Lord Jesus Christ, which according to his abundant mercy hath begotten us *once* again, unto a lively hope *of eternal life* by the resurrection of *the New Creation* Jesus Christ *his Son* from the *spiritually* dead.

4.   *Un*to an inheritance *which is* incorruptible, and undefiled *in any way*, and that fadeth not away; *which is* reserved in heaven for you *who believeth,*

5.   *And* who are kept by the *very* power of God through *Christ's* faith unto salvation ready to be revealed *unto all people* in the last time.

6.   Wherein ye *should* greatly rejoice, though now for a *little* season, if need be, ye are in heaviness through *the* manifold temptations *that ye face.*

7.   That the trial of your *own holy measured* faith, being *so* much more precious than *the cost* of gold that perisheth, though it be tried *even* with fire, might be found, *at the end,* unto praise and honour and glory at the appearing of *the New Creation* Jesus Christ.

8.   Whom having not *personally* seen, ye love. In whom, though now ye see *him* not, yet believing *what ye have heard*, ye rejoice with joy unspeakable and full of glory.

9.   *Ultimately* receiving the end of your faith, *even* the salvation of *your* souls.

10.   Of which salvation the prophets *themselves* have enquired and searched diligently *in the days gone by*, who prophesied of the grace *that should come* unto you *in this age.*

11.   Searching *out* what, or what manner of time the Spirit of Christ which was in them did signify *of*, when it testified beforehand

through them of the sufferings of *the* Christ, and *of* the glory that should follow.

12. Unto whom it was revealed *clearly*, that not unto themselves, but *rather* unto us they did minister the things which are now, *in these days,* reported unto you by them that have preached the gospel unto you with the *power of the* Holy Ghost *who has been* sent down from heaven. *Of* which things the *holy* angels *also* desire to look into.

13. Wherefore gird up the loins of your *renewed* mind, be sober *in your thinking,* and *continue to* hope to the *very* end for the grace that is to be brought unto you at the revelation of *the New Creation Lord* Jesus Christ *from heaven.*

14. *Walk* as obedient children, not fashioning yourselves *once again* according to the former lusts *that ye yielded to* in your ignorance.

15. But as he which hath called *and chosen* you is holy, so be ye *also* holy in all manner of conversation,

16. Because it is written *within the Book of Leviticus,* "Be ye holy, for I am holy."
(Leviticus 11:44)

17. And if ye call *up*on the Father *of lights,* who without respect of persons judgeth

each individual according to every man's *own* work, *and then* pass the time of your sojourning *here on this earth* in *godly* fear *ye shall receive the promised reward.*

18. Forasmuch as ye *should* know that ye were not redeemed with corruptible things, *such as* silver and gold, from your vain *and unprofitable* conversation *which was* **received** by tradition from your fathers,

19. But *ye were redeemed* with the precious blood of Christ *Jesus,* as of a*n innocent* lamb without blemish and without spot.

20. *It was Jesus* who verily was foreordained before the foundation of the world, but was manifest in these last times *of this Probational Period* for you,

21. Who by him do believe in God, that raised him up from the dead, and gave *unto* him glory, *so* that your faith and hope might be in God.

22. Seeing *that* ye have purified your *own* souls in obeying the truth through the *power of the Holy* Spirit unto unfeigned love of the brethren, *see that ye also* love one another with a pure heart fervently,

23. Being Born-Again *from spiritual death,* not of *a* corruptible seed, but of *an*

incorruptible *one*, by the Word of God, which liveth and abideth for ever.

24.　*As it saith in the Book of Isaiah,* "For all flesh is as grass, and all the glory of man *is* as the flower of grass." *(Isaiah 40:6-8)* The grass withereth, and the flower thereof falleth away,

25.　But the word of the Lord endureth for ever. And this is the word which by the gospel is preached unto you.

CHAPTER 2

1.　Wherefore laying aside all malice and all guile, and *all* hypocrisies and envies, and all evil speaking,

2.　As newborn *spiritual* babes, desire the sincere milk of the word *of God*, that ye may grow thereby.

3.　If so be *that* ye have tasted *and seen* that the Lord is gracious.

4.　To whom coming, *as unto* a living stone, disallowed indeed of men, but chosen of God, *and* precious.

5.　Ye also, as *newborn* lively stones, are built up *into* a spiritual house *of habitation for God. And into* an holy priesthood, to offer up spiritual sacrifices, *which are* acceptable to God by Jesus Christ.

6. Wherefore also it is contained *with*in the Scripture, "Behold, I lay in Zion a chief corner stone, elect, *and* precious. And he that believeth on him shall not be confounded." *(Isaiah 28:16)*

7. Unto you therefore which believe *brethren* **he is** precious. But unto them which be disobedient *unto the word*, the stone which the builders disallowed, the same is made the head of the corner,

8. And a stone of stumbling, and a rock of offence, *even to all them* which stumble at the word *of truth*, being *continually* disobedient, whereunto also *even by foreknowledge* they were appointed.

9. But ye *are of* a chosen generation, a royal priesthood, an holy nation, a peculiar people; that ye should shew forth the praises of him who hath called you out of *the kingdom of* darkness into his marvelous light.

10. Which in time past *were* not a people, but *are* now the people of God. Which *at one point in time* had not obtained mercy, but now have obtained mercy.

11. Dearly beloved, I beseech *you* as *being* strangers and pilgrims *on this earth*, abstain from fleshly lusts, which *will* war against the soul,

12. Having your conversation honest among *all of* the Gentiles. That, whereas they *will want to* speak against you as evildoers, they may *instead,* by *your* good works, which they shall behold, glorify *your* God in the day of *his* visitation.

13. Submit yourselves *therefore* to every ordinance of man for the Lord's sake, whether it be to the king, as supreme;

14. Or unto *other* governors, as unto them that are sent by him for the punishment of evildoers, and for the praise of *all* them that do well.

15. For so is the will of God, that with well doing ye may put to silence the ignorance of foolish men,

16. As *spiritually* free *men*, and *yet* not using *your* liberty for a cloke of maliciousness, but *willingly yielding yourselves* as the servants of *the living* God.

17. *Give* honour *unto* all *men*. *Purpose to* love the brotherhood. *Continue to* fear God. *And give due* honour *unto* the king.

18.   Servants, *be* subject to *your* *own* masters with all fear. Not only to the good and gentle *ones*, but also to the froward *and proud*.

19.   For this *is* thankworthy, if a man for conscience toward God endure*s* grief, suffering wrongfully.

20.   For what glory *is it*, if, when ye be buffeted for your *own* faults, ye shall take it patiently? But if, when ye do well, and *then* suffer *for it*, *and* ye take it patiently, this is acceptable with God.

21.   For even hereunto were ye called, because Christ also suffered for us, leaving us an example, that ye should follow *in* his steps.

22.   Who did no sin, neither was guile *ever* found in his mouth.

23.   Who, when he was reviled *by those that hated him*, reviled not again. When he suffered *at the hands of his captors*, he threatened not. But *instead he* committed *himself* to him that judgeth righteously.

24.   Who his own self bare our sins in his own *physical* body on the tree *as a final sacrifice*, that we, being *now* dead to sins, should live *holy and as* unto righteousness. By whose

stripes ye were healed *from all sickness and disease.*

25. **For ye were as** *lost* **sheep going astray, but** *because of the finished work of Christ Jesus on the cross, ye* **are now returned unto the Shepherd and Bishop of your souls.**

CHAPTER 3

1. **Likewise, ye wives,** *be* **in subjection to your own husbands. That, if any obey not** *what the* **word** *of God commands***, they also may without the word be won** *over* **by the** *pure and holy* **conversation of the wives,**

2. **While they behold your chaste conversation** *as it is* **coupled** *with the* **fear** *of the* **Lord.**

3. **Whose adorning** *of beauty,* **let it not be that outward** *adorning* **of plaiting the hair, and of** *the* **wearing of gold, or of** *the* **putting on of** *specific* **apparel.**

4. **But** *let it be* *rather the adorning of* **the hidden man of the heart, in that** *part of our being* **which is not corruptible,** *even the* *ornament* **of a meek and quiet spirit, which is in the sight of God of great price.**

5.   For after this manner in the Old *Testament* time the holy women also, who trusted in God, adorned themselves, being in subjection unto their own husbands.

6.   Even as Sara obeyed Abraham, calling him lord. Whose daughters ye are, as long as ye *continue to* do well, and are not *unduly* afraid with any amazement.

7.   Likewise, ye husbands, dwell *also* with *them* according to *wisdom and* knowledge, giving honour unto the wife, as unto the weaker vessel, and as being heirs together of the grace of life. That *way* your prayers *will* be not hindered.

8.   Finally, *be ye* all of one mind, having compassion one of another. Love as brethren *should*; *be* pitiful, *and be* courteous.

9.   Not rendering evil for *the* evil *that has been done unto thee*, or railing for *the* railing *that ye have received*. But contrariwise, *extend forth a* blessing. Knowing that ye are thereunto called *by God*, that ye should inherit a blessing.

10.   For he that will love *abundant* life, and see good days, let him *purpose to* refrain his tongue from evil, and his lips that they speak no guile.

11.   Let him eschew evil, and do good. *And* let him seek peace, and ensue it.

12.   For the eyes of the Lord *are* *always* over the righteous, and his ears *are* *ever* *open* unto their prayers. But the face of the Lord *is* against *any of* them that do evil.

13.   And who *is* he that will *be able to* harm you, if ye be followers of that which is good?

14.   But, and if, ye suffer for righteousness' sake, happy *are ye* *to be to suffering for the cause of Christ*. And be not afraid of their terror, neither be *ye* troubled.

15.   But sanctify the Lord God *with*in your hearts, and *be* ready always to *give* an answer to every man that asketh you *for* a reason of the hope that is *with*in you, with meekness and fear.

16.   Having a good conscience, that, whereas they *may* speak evil of you, as of *other* evildoers, they may be ashamed that falsely accuse your good conversation in Christ.

17.   For *it is* better, if the will of God be so, that ye suffer for well doing, *rather than* for evil doing.

18.   For Christ also hath once suffered for *all of our* sins, the Just *One dying* for the unjust.

That he might bring us *all un*to **God,** being put to death in the flesh, but quickened *back unto life, in the spirit and in his flesh,* by the *Holy* **Spirit** *of God.*

19. **By which also** *when* he **went** *into the World of Departed Spirits* **and** *suffered for our sins, he also, when he was raised up,* **preached** unto the *captive fallen-angelic* **spirits** *that were* in **prison,** *because they kept not their first estate, but left their own habitation, and cohabitated with Human women, who bore unto them children.*

20. **Which** *at* some *point in* **time were disobedient** *and rebellious unto God, and crossed over species barrier lines,* **when** once the **longsuffering of God waited** *and endured vessels of wrath fitted unto destruction* in the *pre-flood* **days of Noah, while the ark was** *yet* a **preparing, wherein few, that is,** *only* **eight souls were saved by water.**

21. **The** *example of, and* **like figure whereunto** *even* **baptism** *into the body of Christ* **doth also now save us** *from eternal destruction;* (not *just* the putting away of the filth of the flesh, but the answer of a *pure and* good conscience toward God,) by *receiving* the *power of the new birth through* the resurrection of *the New Creation* **Jesus Christ.**

22. Who *himself* is gone into heaven, and is *now seated* on the right hand of God *the Father, who is the Majesty on high;* all angels and *all* authorities and powers being made subject unto him.

CHAPTER 4

1. Forasmuch then as Christ hath suffered for us *when he was yet* in the flesh, *purpose to* arm yourselves likewise with the same mind *that was in him.* For he that hath suffered *for us, and was made to be sin, in the days when he was* in the flesh hath *today* ceased from *being affected in any further way by* sin *because of the work of the cross,*

2. That he no longer should *be subject to* live the rest of *his* time in the flesh to the *sinful dictates of the* lusts of men, but *rather now ought* to *live to fulfill* the will of God.

3. For *in* the time*s* past of *our* life *it* may *have* sufficed us to have wrought the will of the Gentiles, when we walked in *all* lasciviousness, *and* lusts. *In* excess of wine also, *and in* reveling, *and* banqueting, and abominable idolatries.

4.   Wherein *today* they *still* think it strange that ye run not with *them* to the same excess of riot, *and are* speaking evil of *you*.

5.   Who, *in the end,* shall give *an* account to him that is ready to judge the quick and the dead.

6.   For, for this cause was the *blessed* gospel preached also to them that *today* are *now* dead, that they *sadly* might be judged according to men in the flesh, but *because of Christ* live according to God in the spirit.

7.   But the end of all things *within this Probationary Period* is at hand. Be ye therefore sober, and watch unto prayer.

8.   And above all things have fervent charity among yourselves. For *genuine* charity shall cover the multitude of sins.

9.   *Wisely* use hospitality one to another without *displaying any* grudging.

10.   As every man hath received the gift *from God*, **even so** *let him* minister the same one to another, as good stewards of the manifold grace of God.

11.   If any man speak *forth publically*, **let him speak** as the oracles of God *dictate*. If any man minister *to others*, **let him do it** as of the ability which God giveth *unto him*, that God in all things may be glorified through

Jesus Christ, to whom be *all* praise and dominion for ever and ever. Amen.

12. Beloved, think it not strange concerning the fiery trial which is to try you *while you are on this earth*, as though some strange thing *has* happened unto you.

13. But rejoice, inasmuch as ye *know that ye* are partakers of Christ's sufferings. *So that,* when his glory shall be revealed *in its time*, ye may be glad also with exceeding joy.

14. If ye be reproached *by men* for the name of Christ, happy *should ye be*, for the spirit of glory and of God resteth upon you. On their part he is evil spoken of, but on your part he is glorified.

15. But let none of you suffer as a murderer, or *as* a thief, or *as* an evildoer, or as a busybody in other men's matters.

16. Yet if *any man suffer* as a *genuine* Christian, let him not be ashamed. But *rather* let him glorify God on this behalf.

17. For the time *is now come* that judgment must begin at the house of God. And if *it* first *begin* at us, what shall the end *be* of them that obey not the gospel of God?

18. And if the righteous *in Christ Jesus* scarcely be saved, where shall the ungodly and the sinner appear *within the scheme of things?*

19. Wherefore let them that suffer *for Christ* according to the will of God commit the keeping of their souls *to him* in well doing, as unto a faithful Creator.

CHAPTER 5

1. The elders which are among you I exhort, who am also an elder, and a *personal* witness of the sufferings of Christ, and also a partaker of the glory that shall be revealed.
2. Feed the flock of God which is among you, taking the oversight *thereof,* not by constraint, but willingly. Not for filthy lucre *either,* but of a ready mind.
3. Neither as being lords over *God's* heritage *as others,* but being ensamples to the flock.
4. And when the chief Shepherd shall appear, ye shall receive a crown of glory *from him* that fadeth not away.
5. Likewise, ye younger *believers,* submit yourselves unto the elder. Yea, all of you be subject one to another, and be clothed with humility, for *King Solomon saith,* "God resisteth the proud, and giveth grace to the humble." *(Proverbs 3:34)*

6.   Humble yourselves therefore under the mighty hand of God, that he may exalt you in due time.

7.   Casting all *of* your care upon him, for he careth for you.

8.   Be sober, be vigilant, because your adversary the devil, as a roaring lion, walketh about, seeking whom he may devour.

9.   Whom resist steadfast in the faith, knowing that the same afflictions are accomplished in your *other* brethren that are in the world.

10.   But the God of all grace, who hath called us unto his eternal glory by *the New Creation* Christ Jesus, after that ye have suffered a while, make you perfect, establish, strengthen, *and* settle *you*.

11.   To him *be* glory and dominion for ever and ever. Amen.

12.   By Silvanus, a faithful brother unto you, as I suppose, I have written briefly, exhorting, and testifying that this is the true grace of God wherein ye stand.

13.   The *church that is* at Babylon, elected together with you, saluteth you, and *so doth* Marcus my son.

14.   Greet ye one another with a *holy* kiss of charity. Peace *be* with you all that are in Christ Jesus. Amen.

THE BOOK OF
II PETER

CHAPTER 1

1.   Simon Peter, a servant and an *appointed* apostle of *the New Creation* Jesus Christ, to them that have obtained like precious faith with us through the righteousness of God and our Saviour, *the Lord* Jesus Christ.

2.   Grace and peace be multiplied unto you through the knowledge of *our* God, and *also through the knowledge* of *the New Creation* Jesus *Christ* our Lord.

3.   According as his divine power hath given unto us all things that **pertain** unto life and godliness, through the knowledge of him that hath *ultimately* called us to glory and virtue.

4.   Whereby *also* are given unto us exceeding great and precious promises. That by these *promises* ye might be*come* partakers of the divine nature *of our God*, having escaped the corruption that is in the world through lust, *because of the finished work of the cross of Christ.*

5. And beside this, giving all diligence, add to your faith virtue; and to virtue knowledge;

6. And to knowledge temperance; and to temperance patience; and to patience godliness;

7. And to godliness brotherly kindness; and to brotherly kindness charity.

8. For if these things be in you, and abound, they *shall* make *you such that ye shall* neither *be* barren nor unfruitful in the knowledge of our *New Creation* Lord Jesus Christ.

9. But he that lacketh these things is *spiritually* blind, and cannot see afar off *concerning things of eternal value*, and hath forgotten that he was purged from *the bondage of* his old sins.

10. Wherefore the rather, brethren, give *all* diligence to make your calling *of God* and *your* election sure. For if ye do these things, ye shall never fall.

11. For so an entrance shall be ministered unto you abundantly into the everlasting kingdom of our Lord and Saviour, *the New Creation* Jesus Christ.

12. Wherefore I will not be negligent to put you always in remembrance of these

things, though ye *should* know *them*, and *purpose to* be established in the present truth *of the cross.*

13. Yea, *and* I think it meet, *that* as long as I am in this *earthly* tabernacle, to stir you up by putting you in remembrance *of these things.*

14. Knowing that shortly I must put off my tabernacle *of this physical body*, even as our Lord Jesus Christ hath shewed me.

15. Moreover I will endeavour, *through my letters*, that ye may be able *even* after my decease to have these things always in remembrance.

16. For we have not followed cunningly devised fables, when we made known unto you the power and coming of our Lord Jesus Christ, but were *indeed* eyewitnesses of his majesty.

17. For he received from God the Father honour and glory, when there came such a voice to him from the excellent glory *in heaven*, *saying*, "This is my beloved Son, in whom I am well pleased."

18. And this voice which *indeed* came from heaven we heard, when we were with him in the holy mount *at his transfiguration.*

19. We have also a more sure word of prophecy *within the Scriptures.* Whereunto ye

do well that ye take heed, as unto a light that shineth in a dark place, until the day dawn, and the day-star arise in your hearts.

20. Knowing this first, that no prophecy of the scripture is of any private interpretation, *either by the man who was used by God to give it, nor by those in the days in which we live who receive it.*

21. For the prophecy came not in old time by the *personal* will of *any* man. But holy men *called* of God spake *as they were* moved *upon* by the Holy Ghost *himself.*

CHAPTER 2

1. But there were *within those days* false prophets also among the people, even as there shall be false teachers among you, who privily shall bring in damnable heresies, even *going so far as to be* denying the Lord that bought them, and *shall* bring upon themselves swift destruction.

2. And *sadly,* many shall follow their pernicious ways, by reason of whom *even* the *genuine* way of truth, *found only within the death and resurrection of our New Creation Lord Jesus Christ,* shall be evil spoken of.

3. And through covetousness *practices* shall they with *deceivable* feigned words make merchandise of you: whose judgment now *seemingly* of a long time lingereth not, and their damnation *which they justly deserve* slumbereth not.

4. For if God spared not the *rebellious unholy* angels that sinned *in their cohabitating with human women*, but cast **them** down to *the Tartarus compartment of* **Hell**, and delivered **them** *there* into chains of darkness, to be reserved unto judgment,

5. And spared not the old world *from the days of Adam*, but saved Noah the eighth **person**, a preacher of righteousness, bringing in the *second world-wide* flood upon the world of the ungodly,

6. And *then* turning the cities of Sodom and Gomorrah into ashes condemned **them** with an overthrow, making *of* **them** an ensample unto those that after*ward* should live *in an* ungodly manner,

7. And delivered just Lot, *who was* vexed with the filthy conversation of the wicked,

8. (For that righteous man dwelling among them, in seeing *what he did* and hearing *what he did*, vexed *his* righteous soul

from day to day with *all of their* unlawful deeds)

9.   The Lord *indeed* knoweth how to deliver the godly out of temptations, and to reserve the unjust unto the day of judgment to be punished *with everlasting fire*.

10.   But chiefly them that *today* walk after the flesh in *fulfilling* the lust of uncleanness, and   *that*   despise   government. Presumptuous *are they*, *and* self-willed, they are not afraid to speak evil of dignities.

11.   Whereas *holy* angels, which are greater *than men* in power and might, bring not *any* railing accusation against them before the Lord.

12.   But these, as natural brute beasts, made to be taken *for their wicked doings* and *ultimately* destroyed, speak evil of the things that they *are ignorant of and* understand not, and shall utterly perish in their own corruption.

13.   And *they* shall receive the *deserved* reward of unrighteousness, *as* they that count it pleasure to riot in the day time. Spots *they are* and blemishes, sporting themselves with their own *self*-deceivings while they feast with you *in your gatherings*,

14.   Having eyes *and hearts* full of adultery, and that cannot cease from sin beguiling *other* unstable souls. An heart they have exercised with covetous practices, *becoming* cursed children *within the family*.

15.   Which have forsaken the right way *and the deliverance they received through Christ Jesus*, and are gone astray, following the way of Balaam **the son** of Beor, who loved the wages of unrighteousness;

16.   But was *even* rebuked *by the Lord* for his iniquity: the dumb ass *being used as an instrument of God by* speaking with man's voice forbad the madness of the prophet.

17.   These *rebellious individuals* are wells without water, clouds that are carried *about* with a tempest, *and* to whom the mist of darkness *within the Nether World* is reserved for ever.

18.   For when they speak *their* great swelling **words** of vanity, they allure through the lusts of the flesh, **through** *their* **much** wantonness, those *precious souls* that were *once* clean escaped from *all of* them who live in error.

19.   While they promise *to* them liberty, they themselves are *captives, and* the servants of corruption. For of whom a man is

overcome, of the same is he brought in*to* bondage *again.*

20.　For if after they have *once* escaped the pollutions of the world through the knowledge of the Lord and Saviour Jesus Christ, *and* they are again entangled therein and *are* overcome, the latter end is worse with them than the beginning.

21.　For it had been *eternally* better for them not to have known the way of righteousness, than, after they have known it, to turn from the holy commandment delivered unto them *back to disobedience and rebellion.*

22.　But it is happened unto them according to the true proverb, "The dog *is* turned to his own vomit again; and the sow that was *once* washed to her wallowing in the mire." *(Proverbs 26:11)*

CHAPTER 3

1.　This *is the* second epistle, beloved, *that* I now write unto you. *It is* in **both** this *epistle, and the first in the* which I *desire to* stir up your pure minds by way of remembrance:

2.　That ye may be mindful of the words which were spoken before by *all of* the holy prophets, and *also* of the commandment of us the apostles of the Lord and Saviour.

3. Knowing this *very thing* first, that there shall come in the last days scoffers *of the Word of God,* walking after their own lusts.

4. And *boldly* saying, Where is the promise of his coming? For since the fathers fell asleep, all things continue as they were from the beginning of the creation *until now.*

5. For this *reason* they willingly are ignorant of *the fact,* that by the word of *our* God the heavens were of old, and the earth *was* standing out of the water and in the water.

6. Whereby the *pre-Adamite* world *and Social Order* that then was, being overflowed with water *because of disobedience and rebellion,* perished.

7. But the heavens and the earth, which are now *since the seven-day restoration, and the creation of Adam,* by the same word are kept in store, reserved unto *the* fire *which is declared ordained* against the day of judgment and perdition of ungodly men.

8. But, beloved, be *ye* not ignorant of this one thing: that one day *of time* is with the Lord as *if it were* a thousand years, and a

thousand years *of time, is* as *if it were only* one day.

9. The Lord is not slack *my brethren* concerning his promise, as some men *would* count slackness; but is longsuffering to us-ward, not willing that any *intelligent, free-will, moral creature* should perish, but that all *of them which need to,* should come to repentance.

10. But the day of the Lord *which lies just ahead* will come as a thief in the night. *It is* in the which the heavens *themselves* shall pass away with a great noise, and the *temporal physical* elements shall melt with fervent heat. The earth *itself* also and the *sinful* works that are therein shall be burned up.

11. *Seeing* then *that* all *of* these things shall be dissolved, what manner *of persons* ought ye to be in *all* manner *of* holy conversation and godliness, *in these last days in which we live?*

12. *Are ye* looking for and hasting unto the coming of *the Lord, and* the day of *our* God, wherein the heavens being on fire shall be dissolved, and the elements shall melt with fervent heat?

13. Nevertheless we, according to his promise, *are* looking for new *cleansed* heavens

and a new *restored* earth, wherein *will* dwelleth righteousness *for ever*.

14. Wherefore, beloved, seeing that ye look for such things *yourselves*, be diligent *to walk in holiness* that ye may be found of him in peace, without spot, and blameless.

15. And account *that* the *gracious* longsuffering of our Lord *Jesus* *is* salvation *to them that hesitate*. Even as our beloved brother Paul also according to the wisdom given unto him hath written unto you.

16. As *he has declared* also in all *of* *his* epistles. Speaking in them of these *very* things. In *the* which are some things *that he has revealed* hard to be understood, which they that are unlearned and unstable wrest, as *they* *do* also the other scriptures, unto their own destruction.

17. Ye therefore, beloved, seeing *that* ye *should* know *these things* before*hand*, beware, lest ye also *are* being led away *from the truth* with the error of the wicked, *and perchance should* fall from your own steadfastness.

18. But *purpose to* grow in grace, and in the knowledge of our Lord and Saviour *the New Creation* Jesus Christ. U*n*to him *be* glory both now and for ever *more*. Amen.

THE BOOK OF
I JOHN

CHAPTER 1

1.   That which *we know of as The Word, which* was from the beginning, *before all things were created,* which we have *physically* heard *when The Word was made flesh and dwelt among us,* which we have seen with our *own physical* eyes, *and* which we have looked upon, and our hands have handled, of the Word of life;

2.   (For the *source of all* life was manifested *in the flesh,* and we have seen *him,* and bear witness, and show unto you that *in which is* eternal life, which was with the Father *in eternity past,* and was manifested unto us *in these days in which we live.*)

3.   That which we have *physically* seen and heard declare we unto you, *that* ye also may have fellowship with us. And truly, our fellowship *is* with the Father *in heaven,* and with his *Only Begotten* Son, *the New Creation Lord* Jesus Christ.

4.   And these things write we unto you, that your joy may be full.

5.   This then is the message which we
have heard of him, and declare unto you,
that *the One True* God is light, and in him is
no darkness at all.

6.   If we say that we *know God and* have
fellowship with him, and *we continue to* walk in
darkness, we lie, and do not the truth.

7.   But if we *choose to* walk in the light, as
he is in the light, we *then* have fellowship
one with another, and the *shed* blood of
Jesus Christ his Son cleanseth us from all *of
our* sin.

8.   If we say that we have no sin, we *lie
and* deceive ourselves, and the truth is not in
us.

9.   If we *will* confess our sins, he is
faithful and just to forgive us *of our* sins,
and to cleanse us from all unrighteousness.

10.   If we say that we have not sinned, we
make him a liar, and his word is not *dwelling
within* us.

CHAPTER 2

1.   My little children, these things write I
unto you, that ye *choose to* sin not. And if any
man *should fall prey to temptation and* sin, we
have an advocate with the Father *in heaven*,

who is the New Creation **Jesus Christ the** righteous *One.*

2. **And he is the propitiation for our sins. And not for our's only, but also for** *all of the* *sins* **of** *everyone within* **the whole world.**

3. **And hereby we do know that we know him, if we** *obey God and* **keep his** *Royal Law* **commandments.**

4. **He that saith, I know him, and keepeth not his** *Royal Law* **commandments, is a liar, and the truth is not in him,** *because he is not walking in obedience to God.*

5. **But whoso keepeth his** *unchanging* **word, in him verily is the love of God perfected. Hereby know we that we are in him** *because,*

6. **He that saith he abideth in him** *indeed* **ought himself also so to walk, even as he walked.**

7. **Brethren, I write no new commandment unto you, but an old commandment which ye had** *heard right* **from the beginning. The old commandment is the word** *of God* **which ye have heard** *right* **from the beginning.**

8. **Again, a new commandment** *which God hath already declared, but now is fully manifest within the finished work of Christ Jesus* **I** *do* **write unto you, which thing is true in him and in you.**

Because the darkness *which hath exercised dominion in days gone by* is past, and the true light now shineth *within the finished work of Christ.*

9.   He that saith he is in the light, and *continues to* hateth his brother, is in *reality, still in* darkness even until now.

10.   He that loveth his brother *truly* abideth in the light, and there is none occasion of stumbling in him.

11.   But he that *still* hateth his brother is in darkness, and walketh in darkness, and knoweth not whither he goeth, because that *the* darkness hath blinded his eyes.

12.   I write unto you, little children, because your sins *really* are forgiven you for his name's sake, *if you are in Christ Jesus.*

13.   I write unto you, fathers because ye have known him **that is** *the Creator of all things,* from the beginning.

13a. I write unto you, young men, because ye have overcome the wicked one *by being in Christ Jesus.*

13b. Again, I write unto you, little children, because ye have known the Father *even from days gone by.*

14.   I have written unto you fathers, because *I want to remind you that* ye have known him that is from the beginning.

14a. And again, I have written unto you, young men, because ye are strong *and are the hope that God has for today,* and the word of God abideth *and worketh* in you, and ye have overcome the wicked one *through Christ Jesus.*

15.   *My brethren,* love not the world, neither the things *that are* in the world. If any man love the world, *it is evident that* the love of the Father is not in him.

16.   For all that *is* in the world, *and that you allow to affect you, of* the lust of the flesh, and the lust of the eyes, and the pride of life, is not of the Father, but is of the world *system that exists today.*

17.   And the world *system shall* passeth away, and *all* the lust thereof. But he that *faithfully* doeth the will of God abideth for ever.

18.   Little children, it is *indeed* the last time. And as ye have heard that *the* Antichrist *himself* shall come, even now are there many *mini-*antichrists, whereby we know that it is the last time.

19.   They *are those individuals that* went out from us, but they were not of us. For if they

had been of us, they would *no doubt* have continued with us. But *they went out from us*, that they might be made manifest that they were not all of us *but rather were agents working for the kingdom of darkness.*

20.   But ye have an unction from the Holy One, and ye know all things.

21.   I have not written unto you because ye know not the truth. But *I have written* because ye *really do* know it, and that no lie is of the truth.

22.   Who is a liar but he that denieth that Jesus is the Christ *of God*. He is *an* antichrist, that denieth *both* the Father and the Son.

23.   *Because* whosoever denieth the Son *of God*, the same hath not the Father. *But he that acknowledgeth* Jesus Christ **the Son** *of God*, **hath the Father also.**

24.   Let that therefore abide in you, which ye have heard from the beginning. If that which ye have heard from the beginning shall remain in you, ye also shall continue *to abide* in the Son, and in the Father.

25.   And this is the promise that he hath promised us, *even* eternal life *which abides only within his Only Begotten Son, Christ Jesus.*

26.   These *things* have I written unto you concerning them that *attempt to* seduce you.

27. But the anointing which ye have received of him, *by the power of the Holy Spirit,* abideth in you, and ye need not that any man teach you *concerning the things that the Spirit himself would make known.* But as the same anointing *of the Holy Spirit* teacheth you of all things, and is *the* truth, and is no lie, and even as it hath taught you *the truth,* ye shall abide in him.

28. And now, little children, *continue to* abide in him. *So* that when he shall appear, we may have confidence, and not be ashamed before him at his coming.

29. If ye know that he is righteous, ye *should* know that every one that doeth righteousness is born of him.

CHAPTER 3

1. Behold, what manner of love the Father has *demonstrated and* bestowed upon us, that we should be called the sons of God. Therefore, the world knoweth us not *any longer,* because it knew him not, *and we have been recreated into the same image.*

2. Beloved, *right* now are we the sons of God, and it doth not yet appear what we shall be, but we know that, when he shall

appear, we shall be like him, for we shall see him as he is.

3.   And every man that hath this hope in him purifieth himself, even as he is pure.

4.   Whosoever *doth* committeth sin transgresseth also the *Royal* Law, for sin is the transgression of the law.

5.   And ye know that he was manifested to take away our sins, and in him is no sin *at all.*

6.   Whosoever *faithfully* abideth in him sinneth not: whosoever sinneth hath not seen him, neither *really* known him.

7.   Little children, let no man deceive you, he that doeth righteousness is righteous, even as he is righteous.

8.   He that committeth sin is of the devil. For the devil sinneth from the beginning. For this *very* purpose the Son of God was manifested, that he might destroy the works of the devil.

9.   Whosoever is born of God doth not commit sin *within his spirit.* For his seed remaineth in him, and he cannot sin *within his spirit,* because he is born of God.

10.   In this *manner* the children of God are manifest, and *also* the children of the devil. Whosoever *in his behaviour* doeth not

righteousness is not of God, neither *is* he *righteous* that loveth not his brother.

11.   For this is the *same* message that ye heard from the beginning, that we should love one another.

12.   Not as *Adam's son* Cain, *who* was of that wicked one, and slew his brother. And wherefore slew he him? Because his own *sacrificial* works *of bringing an offering which was a product of the curse* were evil, and his brother's *sacrifice of bringing an offering of the blood of a lamb was* righteous.

13.   Marvel not *and do not be surprised*, my brethren, if the world hate you.

14.   We know that we have passed from *spiritual* death unto *spiritual* life, because we *demonstrate that we* love the brethren. He that loveth not *his* brother *continues to* abideth in *spiritual* death.

15.   Whosoever hateth his brother is *in fact* a murderer. And ye know that no murderer *spiritually* hath eternal life abiding in him.

16.   Hereby perceive we the love *of God*, because he *first* laid down his life for us. And we ought *also* to lay down *our* lives for the brethren.

17.   But whoso hath this world's good*s and provisions*, and seeth his brother have *a* need,

and *chooseth to* shutteth up his bowels *of compassion* from him, how dwelleth the love of God *with*in him?

18.   My little children, let us not love *only* in word, neither in *what our* tongue *declares*, but in *the reality of* deed and in truth.

19.   And hereby *shall* we know that we are of the truth, and shall assure our hearts before him.

20.   For if our *very own* heart condemn us *because of what we know about our own shortcomings*, God is greater than our heart, and *truly* knoweth all things.

21.   Beloved, if our heart *shall* condemn us not, *then* have we *great* confidence toward God.

22.   And whatsoever we ask, we *will* receive of him, because we keep his *Royal Law* commandments, and do those things that are pleasing in his sight.

23.   And this is his *stated* commandment, *that Jesus spoke of, and has been established since his resurrection from the dead*, that we should believe on the name of his Son *the New Creation* Jesus Christ, and *then also* love one another, as he gave us *a* commandment *to do so*.

24.   And he that keepeth his *Royal Law* commandments dwelleth in him, and he in

him. And hereby we *shall* know that he abideth in us, by the *bearing witness of the Holy* Spirit, which he hath given *unto* us, *within our spirit.*

CHAPTER 4

1. Beloved, believe not every spirit *manifested of men*, but try the spirits *and put them to the test* whether they are of God. Because *there are* many false prophets *that* are gone out into the world.

2. Hereby know ye the *witness of the* Spirit of God: every spirit *manifested of men* that confesseth that Jesus Christ *is the promised and anointed One of God, and* is come in the flesh is *indeed* of God.

3. And every spirit *manifested of men* that confesseth not that Jesus *is the* Christ *of God, and* is come in the flesh, is not of God. And this is *the influence of* that *spirit* of antichrist, whereof ye have *already* heard that it should come, and even now already is it in the world.

4. Ye are *truly* of God, little children, and have overcome *all of* them, because greater is he that is in you, than he that is in the world.

5.   They are of the world, *so* therefore speak they of the world, and the world heareth them.

6.   We *on the other hand* are of God. He that *truly* knoweth God heareth us, *and* he that is not of God heareth not us. Hereby know we the Spirit of Truth, and the spirit of error.

7.   Beloved, let us love one another. For *genuine* love is of God, and every one that loveth *genuinely* is born of God, and knoweth God.

8.   He that loveth not *genuinely* knoweth not God, for God is love.

9.   In this was manifested the love of God toward us, because that God sent his Only Begotten Son into the world, that we might *become begotten from above, and* live through him *for ever more.*

10.   Herein is *demonstrated* love, not that we loved God, but that he *first* loved us, and sent his Son *Jesus* **to be** the propitiation for our sins.

11.   Beloved, if God *has demonstrated that he* so loved us, we ought also to love one another.

12.   No man hath *physically* seen God *the Father* at any time. If we *manifest* love *for* one

another, *it demonstrates that* **God dwelleth in us, and his love is perfected in us** *by his Holy Spirit.*

13. **Hereby know we that we dwell in him, and he in us, because he hath given us** *the witness* **of his** *Holy* **Spirit.**

14. **And we have seen** *the New Creation Lord Jesus* **and do testify that the Father** *has* **sent the Son** *to be* **the Saviour of the world.**

15. **Whosoever shall confess**, *by the power of the Holy Spirit,* **that Jesus is the Son of God, God** *truly* **dwelleth in him, and he in God.**

16. **And we have known and believed the love that God hath** *shown un***to us. God** *does not just have love, rather he* **is love, and** *because of that* **he that dwelleth in love dwelleth in God, and God in him.**

17. **Herein is our love made perfect, that we may have boldness in the day of judgment. Because as he is** *in his finished resurrection work, legally* **so are we in this world** *right now.*

18. **There is no fear** *at all* **in love, but perfect love casteth out fear. Because** *permitted* **fear hath torment. He that feareth** *demonstrates that he still* **is not made perfect in love.**

19.   *The reason that* we love him, *is* because he first loved us.

20.   If a man say *with his mouth*, I love God, and *yet continues to* hateth his brother, he is a liar. For he that *chooses to* loveth not his brother whom he hath seen, how can he *say that he has* love *for* God whom he hath not seen?

21.   And this commandment *concerning love* have we from him, that he who loveth God *should* love his brother also.

CHAPTER 5

1.   Whosoever *of you that* believeth that Jesus is the *anointed* Christ *that has been sent into this world* is born of God. And every one that *declares that he* loveth him that begat *the Son, should* loveth him also that is begotten of him.

2.   By this we know that we *truly* love the *kindred* children of God, when we love God, and keep his *Royal Law* commandments.

3.   For this is the *demonstrated* love of God, that we keep his *Royal Law* commandments. And his *spoken, love breathed* commandments are not grevious.

4.   For whatsoever is born of God *has legally* overcometh the world. And this is the *observable* victory that overcometh the world, *even* our faith.

5.   Who is he that overcometh the world? But he that *truly* believeth that Jesus is the *Only Begotten* Son of *the One True* God.

6.   This is he that came by water and blood, *even* Jesus Christ. Not by water only, but by water and blood. And it is the *Holy* Spirit that beareth witness, because the *Holy* Spirit is *the Spirit of* Truth.

7.   For there are three *Persons* that bear record in heaven, the Father, the Word, and the Holy Ghost. And these three *Persons* are *the* One *God*.

8.   And there are three that bear witness *here* in the earth, the spirit, and the water, and the blood. And these three agree in one.

9.   If we *normally* receive the witness of men *on given issues*, the witness of God is *much* greater. For this is the witness of God which he hath testified of his *Only Begotten* Son.

10.   He that believeth on the Son of God hath the witness in himself *because of the indwelling of the Holy Spirit*. He that believeth not *what* God *hath testified* hath made him a

liar, because he *chooses to* believeth not the *true* record that God gave of his Son.

11.   And this is the record, that God hath *stated and now made available to us through the finished work of Jesus on the cross:* That he hath given *un*to us eternal life, and *that* this life is in his Son.

12.   He that hath the Son *living within his heart by faith* hath life. He that hath not the Son of God *living within him* hath not life.

13.   These things have I written unto you that believe on the name of the Son of God. *This is so* that ye may know that ye have eternal life, and that ye may *continue to* believe on the name of the Son of God.

14.   And this is the confidence that we have in him, that, if we ask any thing according to his will, he heareth us.

15.   And if we know that he hear us, whatsoever we ask, we know that we have the petitions that we desired of him.

16.   If any man see his brother sin a sin *which* is not unto death, he shall *intercede and* ask, and he shall give him life for them that sin not unto death. There is a sin unto death, *which is blasphemy of the Holy Spirit.* I do not say that he shall pray for it, *for it is not forgivable either in this life, or in the life to come.*

17. All unrighteousness is sin, and *mercifully* there is a sin *that is* not unto *eternal* death.

18. We know that whosoever is born of God sinneth not *on a habitual basis*. But he that is begotten of God *is able to spiritually mature and* keepeth himself, and *in doing so,* that wicked one toucheth him not.

19. We know that we are of God, and *that at this time* the whole world *is still separated from God and* lieth in wickedness.

20. And we know that the Son of God is *surely* come, and hath given *unto* us an understanding, that we may know him that is true, and *that* we are in him that is true *when we are* in his Son Jesus Christ. This is the *One* True God, and eternal life *for those who will receive him*.

21. Little children, keep yourselves from idols.

THE BOOK OF
II JOHN

CHAPTER 1

1. The *apostle and preaching* elder unto the elect lady and her children, whom I *genuinely* love in the truth. And not I only, but also all they that have known the truth *which is declared within the gospel of the Lord Jesus Christ.*

2. For the *Spirit of* Truth's sake, which dwelleth in us *even now*, and shall be with us for ever *even as he has promised.*

3. Grace be with you, *and* mercy, **and** peace, from God the Father, and from the Lord Jesus Christ, *who is* the *New Creation resurrected* Son of the Father, in truth and *in* love.

4. I rejoiced greatly that I found of thy children walking in *the* truth, as we have received a commandment *to love one another* from the Father.

5. And now I beseech thee, *precious* lady, not as though I wrote a new commandment unto thee, but *only* that which we *have* had from the beginning, that we *should continue to* love one another.

6.   And this is *the demonstration of* **love, that** *during the time that we are on this earth, that* **we** *should* **walk after** his *Royal Law* **commandments.** *And* this is the **commandment** *of love*, **that, as ye have** *already* **heard from the beginning, ye should** *purpose to* **walk in it.**

7.   **For many deceivers** *working for the kingdom of darkness* **are entered into the world, who confess not that Jesus** *is the* **Christ** *of the One True God, and* **is come in the flesh** *to fulfill the promises of God.* **This** *individual* **is a deceiver and an antichrist.**

8.   *With purposed soberness* **look to yourselves, that we lose not those things which we have wrought, but** *rather* **that we receive a full reward.**

9.   **Whosoever transgresseth** *and goeth astray*, **and abideth not in the doctrine of** *the finished work of* **Christ, hath not God. He that abideth in the doctrine** *of the finished work of the cross* **of Christ, he hath both the Father and the Son** *living in and walking with him.*

10.   **If there come any** *persons* **unto you, and bring not this** *finished work of the cross* **doctrine, receive him not into** *your* **house, neither bid him God speed** *or God's blessing.*

11. For he that biddeth him God speed *or God's blessing* is *a* partaker of his evil deeds.

12. Having many *more* things to *say and to* write unto you, I would not *at this time* with paper and ink. But I trust to *personally* come to you, and speak face to face, that *your* joy *and mine* may be full.

13. The children of thy elect sister greet thee. Amen.

THE BOOK OF
III JOHN

CHAPTER 1

1.   The *apostle and preaching* elder unto the well-beloved Gaius, whom I *genuinely* love in the truth.

2.   Beloved, I wish above all things that thou mayest *indeed* prosper and be in health, even as thy soul prospereth.

3.   For I *have* rejoiced greatly, when the brethren came *to me* and testified of the truth *of God* that is in thee, even as thou *faithfully* walkest in the truth.

4.   I have no greater joy than to hear that my *spiritual* children walk in truth.

5.   Beloved, *see that* thou doest faithfully whatsoever *the Spirit of Grace directs* thou *to* doest to the brethren, and to strangers.

6.   Which have *publically* borne witness of thy charity before the church. Whom if thou *continuest to* bring forward on their journey after a godly sort, thou shalt do well.

7.   Because that for his name's sake *and by the direction of his Spirit* they went forth, taking nothing of the Gentiles.

8.   We therefore ought to *gladly* receive such, that we might *assist and* be fellow helpers to the truth.

9.   *If you recall,* I wrote unto the church *to do just that*, but Diotrephes, who loveth to *hold the spotlight* and have the preeminence among them, receiveth us not.

10.   Wherefore, if I *personally* come, I will remember his deeds which he *continueth to* doeth. Prating against *the truth of the gospel, and* us, with malicious words. And not content therewith *to only speak against the truth*, but neither doth he himself receive the *newly converted* brethren. And *even* forbiddeth them that would, and casteth *the babes in Christ* out of the church.

11.   Beloved, follow not *that sort of behaviour* which is evil, but *rather follow* that which is good. He that *demonstrates the love of God and* doeth good is of God. But he that *behaveth wickedly and* doeth evil, hath not seen God.

12.   Demetrius *on the other hand* hath *a* good report of all *men*, and of the truth itself. Yea, and we *also* bear record *of this report*, and ye know that our record is true.

13.   I *have* had many things to write *unto you*, but I will not *at this time* with ink and pen write unto thee *concerning them*.

14. But I trust *in the Lord that* I shall shortly see thee *personally*, and we shall speak face to face. *The* peace *of God* **be** *un*to thee. *All of* our friends salute thee. Greet the friends *that are there* by name.

THE BOOK OF
JUDE

CHAPTER 1

1.   Jude, the *half-brother and* servant of *the New Creation* Jesus Christ, and *also the* brother of James, to them that are sanctified by God the Father *through his Holy Spirit*, and preserved in *the finished work of* Jesus Christ, *and* are part of "the **called**",

2.   *Extended* mercy unto you, and peace and love, be multiplied.

3.   Beloved, *before* when I gave all diligence to write unto you of the common salvation *of the finished work of Christ Jesus upon the cross, which belongeth to whosoever will receive it*; it was needful for me to *yet* write unto you, and *to* exhort you that ye should *indeed* earnestly contend for the faith which was once delivered unto the saints.

4.   For there are certain *reprobate* men crept in unawares *even as it was prophesied*, who were before of old ordained to this condemnation. *Even wicked and* ungodly men, turning the *free* grace of our God into *lewd, lustful,* lasciviousness, and denying *the*

truth, and the only Lord God, and our Lord Jesus Christ.

5. I will therefore *endeavour to* put you in remembrance *again*, though ye once knew this, how that the Lord *our God*, having saved the *covenant Jewish* people out of the land of Egypt, afterward destroyed them that believed not.

6. And the *unholy fallen*-angels which kept not their first estate *wherein they were created*, but left their own habitation *within the Realm of the Spirit, and sexually crossed over the species barrier lines to cohabitate with Human women*, he hath, *because of their behaviour*, reserved *them* in everlasting chains, under darkness *within the Nether World compartment of Tartarus*, unto the judgment of the great day.

7. Even as *the inhabitants of* Sodom and Gomorrah, and the cities *round* about them in like manner, *willingly* giving themselves over to *sinful* fornication, and going after *what was to them* strange flesh, are set forth for an example, suffering the vengeance of eternal fire.

8. Likewise also these *filthy* dreamers defile the flesh *that they have been given stewardship over*, despise *those that are in*

dominion *over them*, and speak evil of *legitimate and sincere* dignities.

9.   Yet Michael the Archangel *of God, who is the prince of Israel,* when contending with the devil *himself, when* he disputed about the *burying of* the body of Moses, durst not bring against him a railing accusation, but said *instead,* The Lord rebuke thee.

10.   But these *cursed children* speak evil of those things which they know not. But what*soever things that* they know naturally, as *carnal* brute beasts, in those things they *continue to* corrupt themselves.

11.   Woe unto them! For they have gone in the *same* way *as* of Cain, *Abel's wicked brother.* And *they* ran greedily after the error of Balaam for reward. And *are* perished in the *same* gainsaying of Korah.

12.   These are spots *and blemishes* in your feasts of charity, when they feast with you. Feeding themselves *in your midst* without *any godly* fear. *They are* clouds without *any real* water, carried about of *doctrinal* winds. Trees whose fruit withereth, *indeed* without *any* fruit. *Spiritually* twice dead, *that are destined to be* plucked up by the roots.

13.   *They are like* raging waves of the sea, foaming out their own shame *with every*

reprobate action. **Wandering stars, to whom is reserved** *by our righteous God* **the blackness of darkness for ever.**

14. **And Enoch also, the seventh** *in line* **from Adam, prophesied of these** *before his translation,* **saying, Behold, the Lord cometh with ten thousands of his** *New Creation* **saints,**

15. **To execute** *deserved* **judgment upon all** *who rebel,* **and convince all that are ungodly among them of all** *of* **their ungodly deeds which they have ungodly committed, and of all** *of* **their hard** *speeches* **which ungodly sinners have spoken against him.**

16. **These are murmurers** *and constant* **complainers, walking after their own lusts. And their mouth speaketh great swelling** *words,* **having men's persons in admiration because of** *personal* **advantage.**

17. **But, beloved, remember ye the words** *of warning* **which were spoken before of the apostles of our Lord Jesus Christ.**

18. **How that they told you** *that* **there should be mockers in the last time,** *in which we live,* **who should walk after their own** *selfish* **ungodly lusts.**

19. **These** *shall* **be they who separate themselves** *from sincere men of precious faith, being* sensual, having not the *Holy* Spirit *living within them*.

20.   But ye, *my* beloved, building up yourselves on your most holy faith, *by* praying *at every opportunity* in the *prayer language of the* Holy Ghost.

21.   Keep yourselves *with*in the love of God. *Always* looking for the mercy of our Lord Jesus Christ *that shall lead us* unto *the* eternal life *that was promised.*

22.   And of some *who are struggling* have compassion, making a difference.

23.   And *still* others save with fear, *mercifully* pulling *them* out of the fire*s of Hell*, hating even the garment spotted by the flesh.

24.   Now unto him that is able to keep you from falling, and to present *you* faultless before the *very* presence of his glory with exceeding joy,

25.   To the only wise God *in heaven*, our Saviour, *be* glory and majesty, dominion and power, both now and *for* ever. Amen.

AS A REMINDER ONCE AGAIN: THE PAULINE REVELATION REALITY

Within the plan that was established by Almighty God, the Creator of this universe, from before the beginning of time—the Second Covenant, *"New Creation Project"* of today, affords any Human Being, from any kindred and tongue, living in any nation on the planet, the opportunity to become a:

"Born Again *(John 3:3 & 5)(I Peter 1:23)*, **Recreated** *(Ephesians 2:10)*, **Incorruptible** *(I Corinthians 15:53)*, **Supernatural** *(Matthew 17:20)*, **Resurrected** *(Philippians 3:11)*, **Immortal** *(I Corinthians 15:53)*, **Redeemed** *(Galatians 3:13)*, **More Than a Conqueror** *(Romans 8:37)*, **Blood-Related** *(Ephesians 2:19)*, **Seated at the Right Hand** *(Ephesians 1:20)*, **Conformed to the Image of God-in-the-Flesh** *(Romans 8:29)*, **Administrative** *(Revelation 22:5)*, **Household Member** *(Ephesians 2:19)* of the Family of the Most High God."**

And that is why it is so important that we each need to know, deep within our hearts, just what the *Pauline Revelation* actually says.

Meet the Author

By-The-Book Ministries, Inc. began in 2001 as a teaching outreach. Rob E. Daley has been gifted by God to be able to explain biblical truths in an easy to understand manner.

Many have been blessed by his teaching style.

Rob was saved and filled with the Holy Spirit in 1978 and has been instructed by the greatest teacher of all—the Spirit of Truth Himself. Rob is an ordained minister with the Assemblies of God International Fellowship and has pastored in various churches over the past 34 years.

It is the desire of this ministry to see the body of Christ solidly taught, and grow up into the things of the Lord. Rob is available for seminars, retreats, conventions, etc.

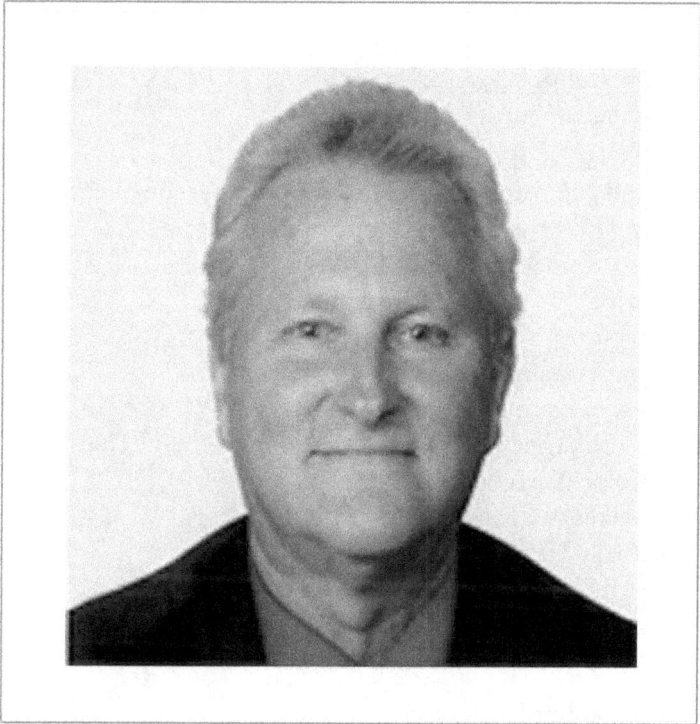

Rob can be reached at:

thedaleys@bythebookministries.org

http://robdaleyauthor.com

BOOKS BY ROBERT E. DALEY

A Case for "Threes"
A Simple Plan . . . of Immense Complexity
Armour, Weapons, And Warfare
from Everlasting to Everlasting
Killer Sex
Life or Death, Heaven or Hell, You Choose!
Raptures and Resurrections
Short Tales
So . . . What Happens to the Package?
Study and Interpretation of The Scriptures Made Simple
Surviving Destruction as A Human Being
The Gospel of John
The Gospel of John (Red Edition)
The League of The Immortals
The New Testament - Pauline Revelation
The New Testament - Pauline Revelation Companion
"The World That Then Was . . ." & The Genesis That Now Is
What Color Are You?
What Makes A Christian Flaky?
What Really Happened to Judas Iscariot?
Who YOU Are in Christ . . . RIGHT NOW!

The Enhancement Series

#1 Book of Ecclesiastes
#2 Book of Daniel
#3 Book of Romans
#4 Book of Galatians
#5 Book of Hebrews

The Deeper Things of God Series

#1 The Personage of God
#2 The Personage of Man
#3 The Personage of Christ
#3 The Personage of Christ

* 9 7 8 0 6 1 5 9 6 8 7 7 3 *